A Collection of the Poetry of Place

Edited by

JOHN WYSE JACKSON

ELAND • LONDON

This arrangement and commentary
© John Wyse Jackson

ISBN 978 1 906011 23 9

First published in October 2008 by Eland Publishing Ltd,
61 Exmouth Market, Clerkenwell, London EC1R 4QL

Pages designed and typeset by Antony Gray
Cover Image: 'Evening on the Liffey' (oil on canvas)
© Nicholas Hely Hutchinson
Printed and bound in Spain by
GraphyCems, Navarra

For my mother,
LOIS WYSE JACKSON,
a Dubliner,
and her seventeen
children and grandchildren,
and in memory of my father,
ROBERT WYSE JACKSON
(1908–1976)

Introduction

YNES MORYSON (1566–1630), secretary of the Lord
Deputy of Ireland, did not much like Dublin – the
mattresses in even the best inns there were always full
of lice. In 1617 he produced a long report, *An Itinerary of an
English Official*, which was full of details and statistics about the
country. It would later be useful to historians. Before he got
going properly with his account of more important matters, he
was concerned to clear up the question of nomenclature. First
he looked at the country as a whole:

> This famous Iland in the Virginian Sea is by old Writers called
> *Ierna*, *Inuerna*, and *Iris*, by the old Inhabitants *Eryn*, by the
> old Britans *Yuerdhen*, by the English at this day *Ireland*, and
> by the Irish Bardes at this day *Banno*, in which sence of the
> Irish word, *Auicen* cals it the holy *Iland*, besides *Plutarch* of
> old called it *Ogigia*, and after him *Isodore* named it *Scotia*.
> This *Ireland*, according, to the Inhabitants, is deuided into
> two parts, the wild Irish, and the English Irish, liuing in the
> English Pale . . .

Then he went on to tackle the capital city:

> The *Eblani* of old inhabited the territory of *Dublin* the fifth
> County, hauing a fertile soyle and rich pastures, but wanting
> wood, so as they burn Turffe, or Seacoale brought out of
> *England*. The City *Dublyn* called *Diuelin* by the English, and
> *Balacleigh* (as seated vpon hurdles) by the Irish, is the cheefe
> City of the Kingdome and seate of Iustice, fairely built,
> frequently inhabited, and adorned with a strong Castle,

fifteene Churches, an Episcopall seate, and a faire College (an unhappy foundation of an Vniuersity laid in our Age), and indowed with many priuiledges . . .

After that, at least his readers would know what he was writing about.

It was writers like Moryson who gave the Irish a bad name. They invented the stage Irishman. When he and other Elizabethan visitors from England (such as the poet Edmund Spenser) were in the country on official (and bloody) government business, the 'Wild Irish' were their main bugbear. Dublin and the eastern counties round it, known as the 'Pale', had for centuries been controlled by the English Crown. Things were quite civilised there, with the 'tame' Irish mingling, apparently happily, with their English superiors. But (except for the more fertile lands of Munster in the south, which were planted with Englishmen and lush dairy grasses) everywhere else on the island was a nightmare. This other Ireland was largely uncharted, full of dangerous bog-holes and trackless mountains, and most of it was covered in forests impenetrable to strangers. The natives knew how to make their way around this wilderness: visitors could imagine weird chieftains and kernes and half-clad children and druids, or whatever they were, at their unearthly rituals in some remote clearing, making uncouth music around Beltane fires and even, perhaps, in Shakespeare's phrase, howling like Irish wolves against the moon. This was an unknown and hostile world, and the English military functionaries and their secretaries feared it. It was from these frustrated English chroniclers, as they attempted and failed to make sense of the Irish problem, that the still-not-quite-extinct stereotype of the savage or comic Irishman sprang.

So, what then of Dublin? With its 'mongrel genealogy', as the poet Edna Longley once put it, this urban centre on the edge of a parochial country has always been a place of contradictions. For hundreds of years it was a capital without being a capital, an enclave of Englishness or mock-Englishness in a land of Irishness. Even now, when the city has grown into a sprawling, prosperous conurbation of glass and concrete and metal, with a central core that (apart from the traffic) hasn't changed all that much for a century, it seems out of place. These days, not so many Dublin people go to church or chapel any more; down the country, where you will find chat in the shops and potholes in the roads, most people still do. But the city's amoeba-like progress, as each year it sends its multi-lane tentacles of tarmac and wire further north and west and south, seems set to engulf all that superstitious rural nonsense before very much longer. In a few more generations, we may all be Dubliners.

Nearly every one of the verses in this book comes from the last three centuries. I have included very little that was written before 1700, nothing by anyone that Fynes Moryson, for example, might have encountered on his travels, and nothing that originally appeared in Irish. Of course Dublin poets (in both languages) existed before the explosion of literary activity that accompanied the work of Jonathan Swift at the beginning of the eighteenth century, but though their work may be of great interest to scholars it is hard to find a home for it in a book for the general reader. Anyway, for reasons that I will touch on below, whichever language those earlier poets used, it was rare for them to write on Dublin.

Indeed, even in the centuries that followed, as I discovered, poems that were actually about Dublin would always be exceptions. While preparing this collection, one of the places I visited in search of inspiration was John Cooke's *The Dublin Book of Irish Verse, 1728–1909*, first published in 1909 by Hodges

9

Figgis & Co., and now more or less forgotten – though completist book collectors value it for three early lyrics by James Joyce. I was sure that among its five hundred and forty entries there would be a good many candidates for me to choose from, but in the event, though there were lots of decent poems written by Dubliners, only a single one even mentioned the city.

I wondered why this should be so, until eventually the penny dropped. It must have something to do with the fact that Dublin has always been somewhere to walk and talk in, rather than to admire. The strikingly elegant Victorian maps of the city show the capital as a smooth oval, a shelled walnut, perhaps, set into the eastern edge of the island. The River Liffey splits this maze of streets horizontally on its way to the sea, and all is bounded by the arcs of the Royal and Grand Canals, with their accompanying North and South Circular Roads. Since then, with the expansion of the suburbs, the cartographic refinement has been lost, but it is hard not to feel that the area within the walnut is still 'Dublin proper', the parts of the city that can reasonably be explored on foot.

Though parts of the city (like a curate's Fabergé egg) are undeniably elegant, its appeal to poets and writers has normally arisen, not from any physical aspect or even any Blakean interior vision, but from the people who live in it. In these pages, accordingly, we will meet a good number of what are usually rather patronisingly known as 'Dublin characters', people who repay your polite interest in them with (in Patrick MacDonogh's wonderful phrase) 'the quick coinage of a laugh'.

Dublin might be as proud as anywhere else – of its handsome squares, its great buildings, its Georgian riverside vistas – but none of its poets has ever written anything comparable to Wordsworth's famous sonnet 'Composed upon Westminster Bridge' (the one that begins 'Earth has not anything to show more fair'). In London, however, Wordsworth was actually able to stop, and muse, and write, and muse again, and in due course, he had his poem. If he had been in Dublin, he would certainly have been interrupted by somebody.

On a personal note, from my garden shed in Wexford I have greatly enjoyed exploring the city on paper as I prepared these pages, especially when I could find a good excuse to spend an hour or two browsing through *Thom's Dublin Directory*. Rather like the internet, a copy of *Thom's* always tells you more than you ever thought you wanted to know. I have three of them on my desk as I write, dated 1911, 1926 and 1944, and I wish I had thirty – though if I did I would need a stronger desk: they're *vast*, probably the thickest books I've ever seen. Printed in double or triple columns using a tiny typeface, each volume has well over a thousand pages – the one for 1926 runs to 2,503.

For a century and a half or so after the first one came out in 1832, these directories were issued each year by the Dublin firm of Alex. Thom and Co. They were repositories of information about Dublin, and essential tools for those who kept the city going – businessmen, traders, politicians, churchmen, educators, advertisers, couriers, members of the police and the civil service. Among other things, they listed all the Dublin streets, all the pubs and shops and offices in each, and they named the owners of all the houses larger than a one-bedroom cottage. Today, they are exciting companions for anyone interested in Dublin's past, its social, economic, educational, ecclesiastical, medical, legal or industrial history, its population trends, its literary figures, its clubs and societies, its families. Or, indeed, almost anything else to do with the city.

Tucked away at the back of each book, after the listings for Yacht Outfitters, Yeast Dealers and Zinc Roof Suppliers, there is a small section entitled 'Dublin Annals'. This idiosyncratic

11

chronology of the city's past grew a little bit longer each year (naturally), but once an entry was in, it was never revised; likewise, omissions were never remedied – there is no mention of the beginning of the Irish Parliamentary tradition in 1264, nor even, surprisingly, of the Great Famine of the 1840s, for example. That said, though the book you are holding claims to be a collection of poems, I take the liberty of beginning with a small selection of prose extracts quarried from the Annals, in the hope that anyone whose grasp of Dublin history is, like mine, a little rusty will find them useful. If not, or if you feel that their accuracy or consistency might be challenged, perhaps you will agree that the entries have a certain poetry all of their own.

Select Chronology

AD 40 to 1916

extracted from Thom's Dublin Annals

40   Eblana, supposed to be Dublin, noticed by Ptolemy, the geographer, as a famous city. It was called by the Irish, Athcliath, or Bally-athcliath, 'the town of the hurdles,' from a ford across the Liffey, then constructed of hurdles.

448   St Patrick converts the king of Dublin, Alphin McEochaid, and his subjects to the Christian faith, and baptises them in a well.

491   St Patrick dies, aged 122 years.

498   Dublin and its vicinity seized on by a fleet of Danes, or Ostmen, who sail up the Liffey, and give the country to the north of the city the name of 'Fingal', or the 'Land of the White Strangers'; and to that of the south, 'Dubghgall', or the 'Land of the Black Strangers'. The city inclosed by them with walls. This event is referred by some writers to the year 838.

The Dark Ages

885   Flan M'Melaghlin, king of Ireland, defeated by the Danes of Dublin.

897   Ireland visited with a plague of strange worms, having two teeth, which devoured everything green in the land.

999   Brian Boru, king of Munster, takes and plunders Dublin.

1014   Battle of Clontarf, in which Sitric, king of the Danes, was defeated, after a long and obstinate engagement, by Brian Boru, who was also killed at the moment of victory.

1169   The Danes of Dublin sue for peace, and give hostages to Dermot and Fitzstephen, the commanders of the English, who landed this year at Bannow, in the county of Wexford.

1172 Henry II holds his court in a pavilion of wickerwork, erected outside the city of Dublin. Here, Strongbow surrenders the government of Dublin to the king.

1262 Contention between the convent of Christ Church and the corporation of Dublin, about the tithe fish of the Liffey.

1286 The citizens of Dublin excommunicated for encroaching on ecclesiastical rights.

1310 A great scarcity, when a cranock of wheat sold for 20s. The bakers were drawn through the city on hurdles fastened to horses' tails, for using false weights, and other frauds.

1331 A great famine relieved by a prodigious shoal of fish, called Turlehydes, being cast on shore at the mouth of the Dodder. They were from 30 to 40 feet long, and so thick that men standing on one side of one of them, could not see those on the other.

1405 Scotland invaded by a fleet fitted out by the citizens of Dublin; after ravaging the coast, they made a descent upon Wales, and carried off thence the shrine of St Cubie, which they deposited in Christ Church.

1452 The Liffey was entirely dry at Dublin for the space of two minutes.

1490 The first importation of claret into Dublin.

1512 The mayor of Dublin sentenced to do penance by walking barefooted through the city in public procession, in consequence of a riot in St Patrick's Church.

1565 John Hawkins, of Sante Fe, New Spain, introduced potatoes into Ireland.

1593 Trinity College opened for the instruction of students.

1623 Proclamation to expel all the Roman Catholic clergy from the kingdom within forty days.

1640 John Atherton, bishop of Waterford, executed at Stephen's-green for bestiality.

1644   Population of Dublin ascertained to be – Protestants, 2,565 males, 2,986 females; Catholics, 1,202 males, 1,406 females: total, 8,159.

1690   James II sleeps one night in Dublin after the battle of the Boyne, after which he proceeded to France. King William attended divine service at St Patrick's Cathedral, to return thanks for his victory at the Boyne. An earthquake felt in Dublin.

1729   The building of the Parliament House, College-green, commenced. Linen scarfs worn at funerals to encourage the linen manufacture.

1739   An intense frost from the end of December to the beginning of February, when the Liffey was frozen over, so that the people amused themselves on the ice. A plague and famine followed.

1773   Act passed for a general pavement of the streets of Dublin. Penny Post-office opened for the city and environs within four miles.

1780   Simpson's Hospital for the reception of poor, decayed, blind, and gouty men, incorporated.

1798   Public soup shops opened by order of Government. Rebellion broke out on the night of the 23rd of May in several counties. Dublin proclaimed under martial law. Several of the leaders of the insurrection executed in Dublin.

1800   The articles of Union laid before the lord lieutenant, by the Houses of Lords and Commons.

1801   Imperial standard hoisted on Dublin Castle.

1802   Act passed for the sale of the buildings of the late Parliament House to the Bank of Ireland.

1803   Insurrection in the city, headed by Robert Emmet, put down the same night it broke out, and several of the leaders executed.

1809   Jubilee for the fiftieth anniversary of the reign of George III celebrated for three days in Dublin.

1822   Riot in the theatre, on the Marquess of Wellesley, the lord lieutenant's first visit thereto, during which a bottle was flung into his Excellency's box.

1834   Population of Dublin, total: 240,273.

1848   May 27. Conviction of John Mitchel for felonious publications in *The United Irishman* newspaper, for which he was forthwith transported to Bermuda Island for fourteen years.

1849   April. The cholera broke out in this month in the city, and continued to rage with intermitting violence till late in October, when the cholera hospitals were finally closed.

       August 5. The Royal squadron, consisting of ten war steamers, including the *Victoria and Albert* yacht, having on board Her Majesty Queen Victoria, Prince Albert, the Prince of Wales, the Princess Royal, Prince Alfred, and the Princess Alice, anchored in Kingstown Harbour.

       August 10. The Queen visited their Graces the Duke and Duchess of Leinster, at their mansion in Carton, where the Royal party partook of a collation; after which, having returned to the Viceregal Lodge, the Royal family proceeded by railroad train to Kingstown, and embarked amidst the acclamations of the assembled thousands.

1867   March 5. Fenian rising in the neighbourhood of Tallaght, put down by the constabulary.

1868   The Vartry Water Works completed this year, when the entire city, together with the Pembroke and Blackrock townships, were supplied with Vartry water, and the old Canal supplies entirely discontinued. The works consist of a large storage reservoir, near Roundwood, in the county Wicklow, which can hold 2,400,000,000 gallons of water, equal to seven months' supply.

1893   Unprecedented drought. Scarcity of water at Round-wood Reservoir. Grand Canal supply resorted to (October 16).

1897   May 11. The New Dublin Fish Market opened.

1899   October 8. Foundation stone of a monument to Charles Stewart Parnell laid in Upper Sackville-street.

1901   January 24. King Edward VII proclaimed in Dublin.

1904   April 26. Their Majesties King Edward VII and Queen Alexandra arrived at Kingstown. Having received addresses from the principal Public Bodies in Ireland, they proceeded by rail to Naas, and attended the Punchestown races.

        December 27. The Irish National Theatre (The Abbey) opened.

1910   May 9. King George V proclaimed in Dublin.

1911   October 1. Great Britain-street renamed Parnell-street.

1912   July 18–19. Rt Hon. H. H. Asquith, MP, Prime Minister, visited Dublin.

1914   August 5. Following the declaration of war by Germany on Russia and the violation of Belgium neutrality, Great Britain declared war on Germany.

        September 18. The Home Rule Bill received the Royal Assent.

1916   On Easter Monday, 24 April, an insurrectionary rising by the Sinn Fein Volunteers began in Dublin. The General Post Office and many other buildings were seized by the rebels, who issued a proclamation establishing 'The Provisional Government of the Irish Republic'. On the 29th the most dreadful conflagration ever seen in Dublin took place. Of the rebels, 15 were sentenced to death . . .

FROM *A Satire on the People of Dublin*

Hail to you, friars, with your cloaks of white!
You have a house at Drogheda, where ropes are made.
You are forever wandering around the place:
You pinch the holy sprinklers out of the churches.
    The one who wrote this piece of literature
    Was undoubtedly a real expert.

Hail to you, holy monks, with your jar
Full of ale and wine, morning, noon and night!
You can really knock back the drink – it's all you care about.
You fall foul of the Benedictine rules, all too often.
    Pay attention to me, the lot of you!
    Obviously you can see that this is crafted with skill.

Hail to you, merchants, with your hefty packs
Of fabrics and other merchandise, and your sacks of wool –
Your gold, silver, jewels, rich marks and pounds as well!
You give very little of it to the poor and afflicted.
    The one who penned this shrewd advice
    Had talent – he was bursting with brains!

Hail to you, tailors, with your sharp scissors!
Endlessly you cut your cloth for ill-made hoods.
Your needles are heated against the midwinter;
Your seams look fine, but they don't last very long.
    The writer who made up this verse
    Stayed wide awake: he got no sleep at all.

Hail to you, skinners, with your steeping-tub!
Anyone who sniffs at it will live to regret it.
You must shite into it during thunderstorms.
You stink out the entire street – a curse on your modesty!
     The one who composed this excellent work
     Deserves to be made king.

Hail to you, bakers, with your little loaves
Of white bread and black bread, lots and lots of them!
You scrimp on the proper weight, against the law of God –
You ought to watch out for the market pillory, I warn you.
     To be sure, no tongue could express
     How well this verse has been put together.

Hail to you, brewers, with your gallons,
Pottles and quarts all around each town!
You displace a lot of it with your thumbs, a sleazy dodge.
You should beware the cucking-stool: the lake is deep
                                   and disgusting.
     It was certainly some scholar
     Who produced this work with such expertise.

Hail to you, hawker women, down by the lake,
With your candles and casks and black cauldrons –
You and your tripes and calves' feet and sheep's heads!
Your inn is foul with your filthy trickery.
     Unhappy the life of the man
     Who is tied to a wife like that.

Perk up, my friends, you've been sitting there too long –
Now speak out for yourselves, have fun, and drink
                                   all you can!

19

You've heard how people spend their lives in this place:
You should drink deep and rejoice – you've got nothing
                                        else to do.
    Now I've come to the end of this song:
    May you be blessed, ever and always.

These extracts come from what may be the earliest surviving poem about Dublin. The verses (put into modern English by the editor) appear in an early fourteenth-century manuscript in the British Library. Nowhere in the work is a place-name actually specified, but the Middle English original contains words that at that date were found only in Ireland, and the settlement described is clearly of some size and importance, so we may be reasonably confident that this is indeed a portrait of medieval Dublin.

Though the anonymous writer trumpets repeatedly about his great poetic skills, his estimation of the city's clerics and tradespeople could scarcely be lower. During the centuries that followed, his opinion was shared by many of the poets who were to write about the citizens – and the fabric – of Dublin.

Description of Dublin

Mass-houses, churches, mixt together;
Streets unpleasant in all weather.
The church, the four courts, and hell contiguous;
Castle, College green, and custom-house gibbous.

Few things here are to tempt ye:
Tawdry outsides, pockets empty:
Five theatres, little trade, and jobbing arts,
Brandy, and snuff-shops, post-chaises, and carts.

Warrants, bailiffs, bills unpaid;
Masters of their servants afraid;
Rogues that daily rob and cut men;
Patriots, gamesters, and footmen.

Lawyers, Revenue-officers, priests, physicians;
Beggars of all ranks, age and conditions,
Worth scarce shews itself upon the ground;
Villainy both with applause and profit crown'd.

Women lazy, drunken, loose;
Men in labour slow, of wine profuse:
Many a scheme that the public must rue it:
This is Dublin, if you knew it.

'In labour slow, of wine profuse' indeed. This sour little portrait of the city in the first half of the eighteenth century is not the most original work to appear in these pages, since it was adapted by an unknown hand from the very similar 'Description of

London' by John Bancks (1709–1751). But prose accounts of the time suggest that the verses were substantially accurate – and indeed, the moans about Dublin enumerated above are not so very different from complaints that were still being uttered two hundred years later.

By now, the old Anglo-Norman town had become a considerable city, with all that the term implies. As the century continued, Ireland's reputation for wild and picturesque beauty spots spread far and wide. Travellers on the alternative Grand Tour might land at Ringsend on the southern bank of the River Liffey, but the moment they found themselves in the dirty streets of Dublin, they hurried out of the city as fast as they could, in search of the magnificent scenes and 'romantick prospects' that they had been told were waiting to be admired almost everywhere else on Erin's green isle. Similarly, when poets noticed their fingers twitching for a quill, they generally avoided the subject of Dublin unless they were feeling in a particularly angry or scornful state of mind.

FROM *Phoenix Park*

James Ward

. . . While thus retir'd, I on the City look,
A Groupe of Buildings in a Cloud of Smoak;
(Where various Domes for various Uses made,
Religion, Revels, Luxury and Trade;
All undistinguish'd in one Mass appear,
And widely diff'ring are united here)
I learn her Vice and Follies to despise,
And love that Heav'n which in the Country lies . . .

    Here careless on some mossy Bank reclin'd,
Lull'd by the murm'ring Stream, and whistling Wind;
Nor poys'nous Asp I fear, nor savage Beast,
That wretched Swains in other Lands infest:
Fir'd with the Love of Song, my Voice I raise,
And woo the Muses to my Country's Praise.

'Phoenix Park' is a lengthy and largely tedious topographical poem that appeared in 1718. Its author, James Ward (1691–1736), was an obscure Church of Ireland clergyman, educated, like almost all obscure Church of Ireland clergy, at Trinity College, Dublin. Until his mid-thirties he was quite productive as a poet, but seems to have withdrawn from writing verse, or at least from publishing it, after he took on the responsibility of Cloyne Cathedral as Dean in 1726.

The Phoenix Park (trueborn Dubliners now use the definite article) dates back to the seventeenth century. It stretched west and north along the River Liffey, just beyond the bounds of the city – and indeed is within them today; in Ireland it is said to be the biggest urban green space in the world (just as O'Connell Street is claimed as the widest main street in the western hemisphere). We may imagine our bucolic cleric gazing over the rooftops from his verdant vantage point, tutting to see the streets shrouded in the black smoke that poured from the chimneys – coal was then Dublin's largest single import. He knows he is safe from snake attack, at any rate, St Patrick having despatched all reptiles from the island some thirteen centuries earlier.

Epigram

on the New Magazine Fort in Phoenix Park

Jonathan Swift

Behold! a proof of *Irish* sense!
    Here *Irish* wit is seen!
When nothing's left, that's worth defence,
    We build a magazine.

In 1735, less than twenty years after the Reverend James Ward reclined on his mossy bank there, the best view of Dublin was commandeered by the military, who built a dump for guns and gunpowder on it. Since then, the Phoenix Park has been something of a cross between a pleasure garden and a parade ground. But we ought to make our way back to the city proper . . .

Jonathan Swift

OYSTERS

Charming oysters I cry:
My masters, come buy,
So plump and so fresh,
So sweet is their flesh,
No Colchester oyster
Is sweeter and moister:
Your stomach they settle,
And rouse up your mettle:
They'll make you a dad
Of a lass or a lad;
And madam your wife
They'll please to the life;
Be she barren, be she old,
Be she slut, or be she scold,
Eat my oysters, and lie near her,
She'll be fruitful, never fear her.

APPLES

Come buy my fine wares,
Plums, apples, and pears.
A hundred a penny,
In conscience too many:
Come, will you have any?
My children are seven,
I wish them in Heaven;

My husband, a sot,
With his pipe and his pot,
Not a farthing will gain them,
And I must maintain them.

HERRINGS

Be not sparing,
Leave off swearing.
Buy my herring
Fresh from Malahide,
Better never was tried.
Come, eat them with pure fresh butter and mustard,
Their bellies are soft, and as white as a custard.
Come, sixpence a-dozen, to get me some bread,
Or, like my own herrings, I soon shall be dead.

Jonathan Swift (1667–1743), Dean of St Patrick's and author of *Gulliver's Travels*, was born and died in Dublin. He wrote these pointed verses inspired by the cries of the street traders he heard drumming up business in the streets around his cathedral. At the time it was rare enough for gentlemen of the church to care about (or even to recognise) the misery that came with poverty; to appreciate the tribulations of working women was almost unique. Swift was practical in his charity – his friend Laetitia Pilkington recalled his story of the bishop who gave a beggar a halfpenny with a blessing and the brigadier who threw him a half-crown with an oath: 'Which,' asked Swift, 'do you think the beggar prayed for at night?' It didn't go unnoticed in the vicinity that the great man whom God had put into their midst always overpaid them when he bought their wares, and that he never tried to convert them to his religion.

For all his notorious grumpiness and impatience, the 'Drapier', as he was called by these Dubliners, earned their lasting affection. On 4 December 1736, *Pue's Occurrences* reported that on the occasion of his seventieth birthday 'there were Bonfires, Illuminations, Firing of Guns, etc. Many loyal Healths were drank; Long Life to the Drapier; Prosperity to poor Ireland; and to the Liberty of the Press.' For many years after his death, tales were still being woven around Dean Swift. They spread throughout Ireland, and two centuries later some of them were brought to light in the far west and south by collectors of Gaelic folklore.

FROM *Stella at Wood Park*

Jonathan Swift

. . . The winter sky began to frown:
Poor Stella must pack off to town;
From purling streams and fountains bubbling,
To Liffey's stinking tide in Dublin:
From wholesome exercise and air,
To sossing in an easy-chair:
From stomach sharp, and hearty feeding,
To piddle like a lady breeding . . .
But now arrives the dismal day;
She must return to Ormond Quay.
The coachman stopt; she look'd, and swore
The rascal had mistook the door:
At coming in, you saw her stoop;
The entry brush'd against her hoop:
Each moment rising in her airs,

She curst the narrow winding stairs:
Began a thousand faults to spy;
The ceiling hardly six feet high;
The smutty wainscot full of cracks:
And half the chairs with broken backs;
Her quarter's out at Lady-day;
She vows she will no longer stay
In lodgings like a poor grisette,
While there are houses to be let.
Howe'er, to keep her spirits up,
She sent for company to sup:
When all the while you might remark,
She strove in vain to ape Wood Park.
Two bottles call'd for, (half her store,
The cupboard could contain but four:)
A supper worthy of herself,
Five nothings in five plates of delf.
Thus for a week the farce went on;
When, all her country savings gone,
She fell into her former scene,
Small beer, a herring, and the Dean . . .

When Swift was appointed to St Patrick's in 1714, Esther Johnson, whom he called 'Stella', was already in Dublin, having some years before taken his advice to come to live in the city. Swift had a problematic relationship with women, but he loved Stella, his 'truest, most virtuous and valuable friend', and he was able to tell her things that as a Dean he could say to nobody else. 'I hate Lent,' he admitted once, 'I hate different diets, and furmity and butter, and herb porridge; and sour devout faces of people who only put on religion for seven weeks.'

In 1719, he composed his first birthday poem for her. In these poems (and in sixty-five off-duty letters he had written to her from London, thankfully preserved as the *Journal to Stella*), his tone of modest, affectionate bantering reveals a charm that was usually obscured by his reputation as an uncompromising satirist. The teasingly jealous couplets above were written in 1723 when Stella had returned to her little house on the Liffey quays after a stay at the mansion of Charles Ford, just outside Dublin.

Soon after writing his epigram on the Phoenix Park Magazine Fort (which is credited with being the last scrap of verse to come from his pen), Swift lapsed into what now appears to have been a form of Alzheimer's Disease. With Stella long dead, his final years were terrible. Seeing few people and recognising fewer, he struggled by the hour up and down the Deanery stairs in a futile effort to regain his health, and the end came slowly: he was dying, as he had predicted, 'first at the top', like a blasted elm tree he had noticed during a walk with friends on the outskirts of the city. After his death, crowds of mourners pushed their way through his front door, bribed the servants for locks of his hair, and in less than an hour, as an early biography put it, 'his venerable head was entirely stripped of all its silver ornaments, so that not a hair remained'.

FROM *Death and Doctor Hornbrook*

Robert Burns

But this that I am gaun to tell
Which lately on a night befel,
Is just as true's the Deil's in hell
      Or Dublin city:
That e'er he nearer comes oursel
      'S a muckle pity.

Even though Robbie Burns (1759–1796) never came to Ireland, he felt it necessary to drag its capital city into his tale of a drunken encounter with the Devil. Poets (and other writers too, God knows) have often found it best to observe Dublin through the bottom of a glass. Still, it can hardly be denied that, since records began, drinking has been the most popular way of passing the time there (particularly when in combination with that even worse vice, talking). The question is asked in James Joyce's *Ulysses* whether it would be possible to cross Dublin without passing a pub. The answer has always been no. In the seventeenth century even the crypt of Christ Church Cathedral was used for the consumption of wines, spirits and tobacco, and official complaints were made about the inebriates below 'pouring either in or out their drink offerings and incense whilst we above are serving the high God'.

The Dublin 'hell' so gratuitously mentioned by Burns was a lane or underground alleyway close to the Cathedral, known for its drinking dens and wine cellars. It was entered through an archway decorated with a bog oak carving of a demon. By the nineteenth century you could rent rooms above it, which (they say) gave rise to small ads in the newspapers, reading:

To be let, furnished apartments in hell.
N.B. They are well suited to a lawyer.

FROM *An Heroic Epistle*

from Donna Teresa Pinna Ÿ Ruiz,
of Murcia, to Richard Twiss, Esq. F.R.S.,
author of
Travels into Spain and Ireland

William Preston

. . . Distracting thought! Some irish damsel's thrall,
Perhaps, this moment, at her feet you fall;
Or on the footstool of her chariot stand,
Sigh, chatter, flirt her fan, and squeeze her hand,
When city belles in Sunday pomp are seen,
And gilded chariots troll round Stephen's-green.*
Ye gods above! – Ye blackguard boys below!
Oh, splash his stockings, and avenge my woe.
Perhaps some siren wafts thee, all alone,
In magic vehicle, to cates unknown;
High low machine, that bears plebeian wight
To distant tea-house, or funereal rite:
Still, as it moves, the proud pavilion nods,
A chaise, by mortals, noddy† term'd, by gods.
Where Donnybrook surveys her winding rills,
And Chapelizod‡ rears her sunny hills;
Thy sumptuous board the little loves prepare,

---

* Stephen's-green, a place of public resort, especially on Sundays, when
the nobility and gentry take the air there, and parade in their carriages.
For a description of it, *vide* Twiss's *Tour in Ireland*.
† Noddy, for a description of this vehicle, *vide* the same work.
‡ Donnybrook, Chapelizod, names of pleasant villages in the neigh-
bourhood of Dublin.

And sally lun,[§] and saffron cakes are there.
Blest saffron cakes! from you may Dublin claim
Peculiar pleasure and peculiar fame.
Blest cakes! plump, yellow, tempting, as the breast
Of gypsy, heaving thro' the tatter'd vest!
Once, smocks[¶] alone, neglected saffron dy'd,

§ Sally lun, a particular species of large cakes, probably so called from
the first inventor of them. At the time alluded to by our author, these
cakes were in much request in Dublin:

> There was then a person who profest to have a secret exclusive
> recipe for making, dressing and cutting them up. – When one of
> his cakes was bespoke, he used to convey it and himself in a sedan-
> chair, and prepare it to be served up, with much self-importance
> and mysterious solemnity. – Such anecdotes may seem trifling to
> superficial minds untouched by the venerable love of antiquarian
> research: but to those who have a proper sense of things, they are
> of the utmost importance.   STEEVENS

> These cakes are among the few manufactures which flourish in the
> neglected kingdom of Ireland. They are peculiar to Ireland, and not
> only to Ireland, but to one particular town in Ireland, namely
> Dublin. How this exclusive privilege was obtained, whether by
> prescription or grant, and, if by grant, whether by charter of patent,
> I have not been able to discover, though I have employed many
> years in the research, and all the ardour which such an interesting
> inquiry deserves.
>   Probably, if so many records in Birmingham tower had not been
> destroyed by fire, early in this century, I might have been successful;
> but, to the irreparable loss and everlasting regret of all true anti-
> quarians, that flame, when extinguished, most unhappily left
> posterity in the dark as to many points of curious investigation;
> nor have I found one spark to throw a light on the present obscure
> subject.   SIR J. HAWKINS

¶ Smocks, alluding to the custom which anciently prevailed among the
Irish of dying their linen with saffron.

Unwashed to wear them was the maiden's pride;
The generous drug, more honour'd than of yore,
Now fills the bellies it adorn'd before . . .

We are now firmly in the late eighteenth century. William Preston (1753–1807) was a Dublin poet, playwright, barrister, and, needless to say, member of a convivial literary drinking club, the Monks of the Screw. He liked writing poetry, but he liked writing satirical verse more. He even teased the Provost of his *alma mater*, Trinity College, Dublin, in heroic couplets so unflattering that they were collected in a successfully scandalous volume called *Pranceriana*.

When Richard Twiss, a traveller and jobbing writer from England, published his *Tour in Ireland 1775*, everyone in Dublin hated it. Preston immediately wrote the verses above, using the name of a lady whom Twiss had apparently abandoned in Spain, lovelorn and jealous. He followed it with a reply that claimed to come from Twiss. Preston then had his verses circulated in Dublin, passing them off as having been issued by Twiss himself. After this episode, the unfortunate Twiss lapsed into silence for almost twenty years, during which time, as the *Dictionary of National Biography* puts it, he 'devoted himself to literature and fine arts and to speculations endeavouring to manufacture paper out of straw, whereby he seriously impaired his fortune'.

The notes following the lines above are Preston's. Though he did not explain the now obscure word 'cates' (it meant 'sweetmeats' or 'tasty titbits'), he followed Twiss's practice of spicing his work with memorably uninteresting footnotes. These teases were sometimes 'taken' from other authorities, such as George Steevens, an early annotator of Shakespeare, or the first biographer of Dr Johnson, Sir John Hawkins. They all were quite unnecessary, and delightful.

*from a Female Rabbi in Jerusalem
to a Celebrated Buck in Ireland*

Thomas Dermody

> . . . But ah! my dearest, let not gypsies lead
> Thy vagrant wand'rings to the rural mead;
> Let dire Drumcondra e'er unheeded lie,
> Though teapots, cups and saucers, court the eye . . .

Another warning against the siren call of tea and buns in Dublin's outlying hamlets. Until the nineteenth century, the city, for all its importance, was a small one compared with what it was to become; the villages that surrounded it (Donnybrook, Drumcondra, Chapelizod and the like) were still part of rural Ireland, even though they might boast teashops, bagnios, public pleasure gardens and similar amenities tempting to the leisured or libertine classes.

Thomas Dermody (1775–1802) was one of the oddest of Irish poets – a calling in which oddness has never been in short supply. Following his father's example, he was by all accounts a confirmed alcoholic before he reached his teens; but then again, most of his best work was written long before he was twenty. The snippet above comes from a verse from a fictional lady pining in foreign parts. Beginning 'Dear hapless youth! and object of my flame', the poem must surely be modelled on William Preston's successful hoax a decade or two before.

To be on the safe side, Dermody wrote his own epitaph a little earlier than most poets tend to do. It included the lines:

As a *man*, did I say? when death shifted the scene,
A giant of genius, he was *not fifteen*.
Him whom living ye nourish'd with ink and with bays,
To others the profit, to him the mere praise . . .
Oh! now that you fear nor his smiles nor his lashes,
Be candid for once, and disturb not his ashes.

In 1806 his first and last biographer disapprovingly commented on this and similar poetic excursions, saying that they displayed 'that partiality to low company and drinking which often obscured his splendid genius, and ultimately brought him to an early grave'. Dermody's last chance to give up drink and make something of himself came when he joined the 108th Regiment of the Line, and he soon won a commission as second lieutenant (most suitably, in the wagon corps). But after being wounded abroad, he went back to the bottle, and died aged twenty-seven 'in a wretched hovel near Sydenham, London'. His so-called 'last words' have come down to us as: 'I am vicious [*i.e.* depraved, immoral] because I like it.'

FROM *The Sprig of Shillelah*

Edward Lysaght

Who has e'er had the luck to see Donnybrook Fair?
An Irishman, all in his glory, is there,
    With his sprig of shillelah and shamrock so green!
His clothes spick and span new, without e'er a speck,
A neat Barcelona tied round his white neck;
He goes to a tent, and he spends half-a-crown,
He meets with a friend, and for love knocks him down,
    With his sprig of shillelah and shamrock so green!

At evening returning, as homeward he goes,
His heart soft with whisky, his head soft with blows
   From a sprig of shillelah and shamrock so green!
He meets with his Sheelah, who, frowning a smile,
Cries, 'Get ye gone, Pat,' yet consents all the while.
To the priest soon they go, and nine months after that,
A baby cries out, 'How d'ye do, father Pat,
   With your sprig of shillelah and shamrock so green?'

By the time that 'Pleasant Ned' Lysaght (1763–1810) wrote
these jolly 'Oirish' verses, the ancient horse market just south of
the city on the banks of the River Dodder had become proverbial
for fighting, wenching and general alcoholic depravity. In the
1850s, with Donnybrook village now a suburb of Dublin, the
fair was abolished after residents objected to the annual influx of
prostitutes and conmen who, when they weren't extracting cash
from a gullible public, were reputed to spend the fortnight
dancing and belabouring each other with their blackthorn
cudgels ('shillelahs'). Today there are occasional calls for the
event to be revived as a tourist attraction.

The Night before Larry was Stretched

The night before Larry was stretched,
   The boys they all paid him a visit;
A bait in their sacks, too, they fetched;
   They sweated their duds till they riz it:
For Larry was ever the lad,
   When a boy was condemned to the squeezer,
Would fence all the duds that he had
   To help a poor friend to a sneezer,
     And warm his gob 'fore he died.

The boys they came crowding in fast,
    They drew all their stools round about him,
Six glims round his trap-case were placed,
    He couldn't be well waked without 'em.
When one of us asked could he die
    Without having duly repented,
Says Larry, 'That's all in my eye,
    And first by the clergy invented,
        To get a fat bit for themselves.'

'I'm sorry, dear Larry,' says I,
    'To see you in this situation;
And, blister my limbs if I lie,
    I'd as lieve it had been my own station.'
'Ochone! it's all over,' says he,
    'For the neckcloth I'll be forced to put on,
And by this time tomorrow you'll see
    Your poor Larry as dead as a mutton,
        Because why, his courage was good.

'And I'll be cut up like a pie,
    And my nob from my body be parted.'
'You're in the wrong box, then,' says I,
    'For blast me if they're so hard-hearted:
A chalk on the back of your neck
    Is all that Jack Ketch dares to give you;
Then mind not such trifles a feck,
    For why should the likes of them grieve you?
        And now, boys, come tip us the deck.'

The cards being called for, they played,
    Till Larry found one of them cheated;
A dart at his napper he made

(The boy being easily heated):
'Horo! by the hokey, you thief,
   I'll scuttle your nob with my daddle!
You cheat me because I'm in grief,
   But soon I'll demolish your noddle,
      And leave you your claret to drink.'

Then the clergy came in with his book,
   He spoke him so smooth and so civil;
Larry tipped him a Kilmainham look,
   And pitched his bag wig to the devil;
Then sighing, he threw back his head
   To get a sweet drop of the bottle,
And pitiful sighing, he said,
   'O the hemp will be soon round my throttle,
      And choke my poor windpipe to death.

'Though sure it's the best way to die,
   O! the devil a better a-livin',
For when the dam gallows is high
   Your journey is shorter to Heaven:
But what harasses Larry the most,
   And makes his poor soul melancholy,
Is to think of the time when his ghost
   Will come in a sheet to sweet Molly — ;
      O, sure it will kill her alive!'

So moving these last words he spoke,
   We vented our tears in a shower;
Meself, sure I thought my heart broke,
   To see him cut down like a flower.
On his travels we watched him next day;

O, the throttler! I thought I could kill him;
But Larry not one word did say,
   Nor changed till he came to King William,
      Then, musha, his colour grew white.

When he came to the old nubbling-cheat,
   He was tucked up so neat and so pretty,
The rumbler jogged off from his feet,
   And he died with his face to the city;
He kicked, too – but that was all pride,
   For soon you might see 'twas all over;
Soon after, the noose was untied,
   And at darky we waked him in clover
      And sent him to take a ground sweat.

This energetic account of the last hours of a felon's life has been a Dublin favourite for over two centuries. Though it uses the occasional puzzling nonce-word, it is not hard to make out what is going on, particularly after the first verse – in which Larry Coffey, waiting in prison to be hanged, is visited by his cronies with bottles. They have 'sweated their duds' (pawned their clothes) to raise the drinking-money, as Larry has done on similar occasions previously. At the end of the song, they follow the execution party past Grinling Gibbons's statue of King Billy in Dame Street, and at the gallows (the 'nubbling-cheat'), they claim Larry's dead body. That night in a nearby field they hold one last session with him, his own wake, before they dig a hole and pop his body into the great pawnshop underground.

Such was the popularity of 'Larry' when it appeared – probably not long before the end of the eighteenth century – that it gave rise to several ghoulish spinoffs adding to the story. Titles included 'Larry's Ghost', 'Mrs Coffey' and 'The Kilmainham

Minuet' – *i.e.* the dance that a hanged man does at the end of the rope. Like the first one, each of these songs appends an extra (ninth) line to each verse, known as the 'ceangal', or *envoi*, a curious but effective device borrowed from the Gaelic tradition.

Common to all the 'Larry' songs is a stoical acceptance that the possibility of being hanged for some crime or other is just one of the hazards of life in Dublin, and that there is not a great deal that can be done about it.

Mo Craoibhín Cnó

Edward Walsh

My heart is far from Liffey's tide
   And Dublin town;
It strays beyond the southern side
   Of Knockmealdown,
Where Cappoquin hath woodlands green,
   Where Avonmore's waters flow,
Where dwells unsung, unsought, unseen,
   Mo craoibhín cnó,
Low clustering in her leafy screen,
   Mo craoibhín cnó!

The high-bred dames of Dublin town
   Are rich and fair,
With wavy plume and silken gown,
   And stately air;
Can plumes compare thy dark brown hair?
   Can silks thy neck of snow?
Or measur'd pace thine artless grace,
   Mo craoibhín cnó,

When harebells scarcely show thy trace,
  Mo craoibhín cnó?

I've heard the songs by Liffey's wave
  That maidens sung –
They sung their land the Saxon's slave,
  In Saxon tongue –
Oh! bring me here that Gaelic dear
  Which cursed the Saxon foe,
When thou didst charm my raptured ear,
  Mo craoibhín cnó!
And none but God's good angels near,
  Mo craoibhín cnó!

I've wandered by the rolling Lee!
  And Lene's green bowers –
I've seen the Shannon's wide-spread sea,
  And Limerick's towers –
And Liffey's tide, where halls of pride
  Frown o'er the flood below;
My wild heart strays to Avonmore's side,
  Mo craoibhín cnó!
With love and thee for aye to bide,
  Mo craoibhín cnó!

Edward Walsh (1805–1850), though born in Ulster, was at heart
a Corkman. He has always been admired for his subtly musical
translations from Irish rather than for his original poetry. In
some ways it is odd that he became so enthusiastic a translator,
for he disapproved of 'the mere English-speaking Irish', whose
language was 'as the chirpings of a cock-sparrow on the house-
roof to the soft cooing of the gentle cushat by the southern
Blackwater'.

Walsh's education took place in an illegal hedge-school, where he fell in love with the native tongue; he himself went on to become a teacher, not only under hedges but after 1831, when national education for Roman Catholics was brought in, in the national schools. Unfortunately, none of these jobs lasted long, for he was constantly being sacked or imprisoned (or both) for publishing seditiously nationalistic articles and verses. Between teaching posts, one short interlude in alien Dublin, working as a journalist and corn clerk, was enough for him, and he scurried back to Cork to instruct young prisoners in the jail on Spike Island. After yet another dismissal, for interviewing the Young Irelander, John Mitchel, who was being held there, he ended his days as schoolmaster in the Cork workhouse.

In this version of a popular Irish original, Walsh exercises with relish a Corkonian animus against all things Dublinish. Once again the city, with its foreign fripperies, is unfavourably contrasted with the true Ireland, the pure Gaelic-speaking countryside, where there are proper honest-to-goodness colleens to worship. *Craoibhín cnó* is variously defined in Father Dinneen's delightful Irish dictionary as 'a cluster of nuts; a row of turf-sods put standing upright around and over the mouth of a creel to keep in the smaller peat; a fair maiden'. The first and last of these are probably the ones to bear in mind here.

Dublin City

Charles Lever

Och, Dublin city, there is no doubtin',
    Bates every city upon the say;
'Tis there you'd hear O'Connell spoutin',
    An' Lady Morgan makin' tay.
For 'tis the capital o' the finest nation,
    Wid charmin' pisintry upon a fruitful sod,
Fightin' like divils for conciliation,
    An' hatin' each other for the love of God.

Like many before and since, it was at Trinity College, Dublin, that
Charles Lever (1806–1872) found his natural métier: carousing
all night, eating and dancing and drinking, and in the morning
riding dangerously and noisily through the streets of the city.
Strangers passing through Front Square noticed him surrounded
by laughing friends, with his head of shoulder-length curls, and
his imposing figure clad top to toe in Lincoln green. Sometimes
his talk was so wild and fanciful that people assumed that he had
been taking opium. Sometimes, indeed, he had. To pay for the
booze, the clothes, the balls, the oysters and devilled kidneys,
the drugs, the horses and the gambling – he would eventually
lose several fortunes playing whist – he graciously accepted large
subventions from his proud father, and when these ran out he
not only wrote ballads, but sang them at street corners and sold
them to passers-by; one night with a friend he is said to have
netted thirty shillings in halfpence. Lever's days as a student
were the best of his life.

Years later, in his novels (which were once very popular, and
ought to be so again), he often revisited this time. The Dublin

street-singer Rhoudlum was one he remembered. She was, he wrote, 'a fiend-like old woman, with one eye, and a voice like a cracked bassoon. She was dressed in a soldier's cast-off coat and a man's hat, and either in face or costume had few feminine traits. She was followed by a mob of admiring amateurs, who seemed to form her bodyguard and her chorus.'

Siberia

James Clarence Mangan

In Siberia's wastes
    The Ice-wind's breath
Woundeth like the toothèd steel.
Lost Siberia doth reveal
    Only blight and death.

Blight and death alone.
    No Summer shines.
Night is interblent with Day.
In Siberia's wastes alway
    The blood blackens, the heart pines.

In Siberia's wastes
    No tears are shed,
For they freeze within the brain.
Nought is felt but dullest pain,
    Pain acute, yet dead;

Pain as in a dream,
    When years go by
Funeral-paced, yet fugitive,
When man lives, and doth not live,
    Doth not live – nor die.

In Siberia's wastes
    Are sands and rocks.
Nothing blooms of green or soft,
But the snowpeaks rise aloft
    And the gaunt ice-blocks.

And the exile there
    Is one with those;
They are part, and he is part,
For the sands are in his heart,
    And the killing snows.

Therefore, in those wastes
    None curse the Czar.
Each man's tongue is cloven by
The North Blast, that heweth nigh
    With sharp scymitar.

And such doom each drees,
    Till, hunger-gnawn,
And cold-slain, he at length sinks there,
Yet scarce more a corpse than ere
    His last breath was drawn.

James Clarence Mangan (1803–1849) was born in Dublin and, unlike Swift and Sheridan and Wilde and Joyce and Yeats and Beckett, he rarely ventured out of the city, remaining a Dubliner among Dubliners. A shy individual, he never married, and few people knew him very well, but many spoke of the witch's hat and cloak he wore, the outsize green spectacles, the *pair* of enormous umbrellas under his arm, the ever-present bottle of light-brown liquid that he claimed was tar-water. During the 1830s or 1840s, you might glimpse him browsing along the

45

bookstalls on Batchelor's Walk beside the river, or dodging like a twilight wraith into a tavern in Bride Street. These sightings became part of the lore of the city. Someone remembered spotting his gaunt figure halfway up a ladder in a library, the pinched, wax-pale countenance, old at thirty, still bearing 'traces of nobility and poetic sensibility'. Tales were told of how the mad opium-eating poet hastened his early death by falling into a big hole in the road after closing time. Even during his lifetime Mangan's desperate begging letters had become relics; after it they comprised the bulk of his surviving correspondence.

So what are his chilling lines about Siberia doing in a book of Dublin poetry? They were published on 18 April 1846 in the *Nation*, the newspaper and cultural journal of the nationalist Young Irelanders, which in the previous week's issue had reported that some anti-Czarist Polish leaders had been banished to hard labour in Siberia. Though the less separatist readers of the *Nation* may not have realised it, Mangan tackles several subjects in his allusive poem, but Siberia is not really one of them.

The story gave Mangan a metaphor to address issues closer to home: silence, exile, blight and death, the four hard faces of Ireland's Armageddon. The potato blight had struck six months before, and Famine now had Ireland in its terrible grip. Since the Act of Union in 1800, when Dublin had been stripped of its parliament (versions of which had been operating since the thirteenth century), the city had become a serf, a creature of the English crown, with political life frozen and free speech silenced. Without real executive power, Irish leaders could do little to alleviate the suffering – while for the thousands currently fleeing the country, weakened by hunger and disease, exile would actually mean death. Like all great works of art, 'Siberia' can be approached in many ways.

It may also be read as a personal cry of pain from the poet

himself, ill, addicted, often hungry and cold, isolated in a grey city on a green island. Three years later, James Clarence Mangan lay dead in the Meath Hospital. He was forty-six. Five people came to his funeral – some say three.

FROM *St Patrick was a Gentleman*

Michael J. Moran (Zozimus)

St Patrick was a gentleman,
    He came of decent people:
He built a church in Dublin town,
    And on it put a steeple.
His father was a Gallagher,
    His mother was a Brady,
His aunt was an O'Shaughnessy,
    His uncle an O'Grady.

CHORUS

So success attend St Patrick's fist,
    For he's a saint so clever;
Oh! he gave the snakes and toads a twist,
    And banish'd them for ever! . . .

One edition of the *Oxford Dictionary of Quotations* says that it was a Henry Bennett who wrote the comic ballad that starts with the verse above, when every Dubliner worthy of the name knows that it was by Zozimus, the blind singer and reciter extraordinaire of Dublin, born Michael Moran (1796–1846). He was even better known than his female counterpart, Rhoudlum.

It appears to have been the fate of Moran to be impersonated. Once, for a wager, an eminent local actor disguised himself in the familiar uniform of frieze coat, cape, old corduroys, brogues and stick and began reciting for a crowd on the ballad-singer's pitch at Essex Bridge. When Moran appeared with his own crowd and began to recite as well, the actor called to his supporters to 'give him a grip of that villain, and he'd soon let him know who the imposhterer was!' To the general relief, when the two Zozimi were brought together, the false one confessed to the apoplectic real one, handed over the coins he had feloniously collected, and went off to claim the winnings on his bet.

Dickey and the Yeomen

Zozimus (Michael J. Moran)

At the dirty end of Dirty lane,
Liv'd a dirty cobbler, Dick McClane;
His wife was, in the old king's reign,
    A stout brave orange-woman.

On Essex bridge she strained her throat,
And six-a-penny was her note;
But Dickey wore a bran-new coat,
    He got among the yeomen.

He was a bigot, like his clan,
And in the streets he wildly sang,
O Roly, toly, toly raid,
    With his old jade.

Of the comic verses that Zozimus wrote at the expense of fellow citizens whom he disliked, this is one of the few to have survived. Clearly, McClane was a pill, toadying up to respectable gentlemen far above his station, and forcing his unfortunate wife, her voice ruined by years of street-trading, to sing with him for their supper. It cannot have pleased Zozimus for their caterwauling at the bridge must have grossly interfered with his own performances there.

Zozimus died in April 1846. He was given the mother and father of all wakes, attended by a host of fiddlers and singers and storytellers, and the next morning, a bitterly cold day, a large crowd followed his hearse to the cemetery in Glasnevin. 'Bad cess to him,' one mourner complained; 'I wish he'd held out another month until the weather got dacent.'

Naturally, it wasn't very long before a man called M'Grane was in position at Essex Bridge, announcing that the dead man was a fake, and that he had been the real Zozimus all the time.

The Rocky Road to Dublin

In the merry month of June, from my home I started,
Left the girls of Tuam nearly broken-hearted,
Saluted father dear, kissed my darlin' mother,
Drank a pint of beer my grief and tears to smother.
Then off to reap the corn, and leave where I was born,
I cut a stout blackthorn to banish ghost and goblin,
In a bran-new pair of brogues I rattled o'er the bogs,
And frightened all the dogs on the rocky road to Dublin.

CHORUS

One, two, three, four, five,
Hunt the hare and turn her
Down the rocky road and all the ways to Dublin,
Whack-fol-lol-de-ra.

In Mullingar that night I rested limbs so weary,
Started by daylight next mornin' light and airy;
Took a drop of the pure, to keep my heart from sinkin',
That's an Irishman's cure, whene'er he's on for drinking.
To see the lassies smile, laughing all the while,
At my curious style, 'twould set your heart a-bubblin'.
They ax'd if I was hired, the wages I required,
Till I was almost tired of the rocky road to Dublin.

In Dublin next arrived, I thought it such a pity,
To be so soon deprived a view of that fine city.
Then I took a stroll all among the quality,
My bundle it was stole in a neat locality;
Something crossed my mind, when I looked behind
No bundle could I find upon my stick a-wobblin'.
Enquirin' for the rogue, they said my Connacht brogue
Wasn't much in vogue on the rocky road to Dublin.

From there I got away, my spirits never failin',
Landed on the quay as the ship was sailin';
Captain at me roared, said that no room had he,
When I jumped aboard, a cabin found for Paddy
Down among the pigs; I played some funny rigs,
Danced some hearty jigs, the water round me bubblin',
But when off Holyhead, I wished myself was dead,
Or better far instead, on the rocky road to Dublin.

The boys of Liverpool, when we safely landed,
Called myself a fool, I could no longer stand it;
Blood began to boil, temper I was losin',
Poor ould Erin's isle they began abusin'.
'Hurrah my soul!' sez I, my shillelagh I let fly;
Some Galway boys were by, saw I was a hobble in,

Then with a loud hurray, they joined in the affray.
We quickly cleared the way, for the rocky road to Dublin.

Once more, Dublin gets a bad press here. The city is seen as snobbish and unprincipled, but it is a necessary stage on the journey between the certainty of poverty in County Galway and the hope of riches offered by emigration. Still, when our hero finds himself in England, national pride asserts itself: perhaps Dublin doesn't seem such a bad place after all.

The song comes from one of the printed ballad broadsheets that were sold in the streets of Dublin and other centres during the eighteenth and nineteenth centuries. Hundreds of ballads were run off on a host of little presses: rumour has it that the earliest works of Oliver Goldsmith were anonymous songs for these broadsheets, written to supplement his sizarship to Trinity. At night, a biographer tells us, the young poet would sometimes slip out of the college, 'creeping within dark shadows of the ill-lighted streets' to find out how the balladeer's audiences were reacting to his latest song.

'The Rocky Road to Dublin' has remained popular, and has been recorded many times, partly because the instantly recognisable tune is the best-known example of a 'slip jig'. One highly recommended, if unlikely, version features the Rolling Stones, guesting on an album by the Chieftains, in which the virtuoso fiddle-playing of Ireland's leading group of traditional musicians duels manfully with electric-guitar riffs from 'Satisfaction', while Charlie Watts maintains an insistent Celtic tattoo in the background.

The Return

John Francis O'Donnell

Once more the red familiar streets
    Are round me; and the Irish sky,
Filled with its myriad cloudy feats,
    Bends deep above. The sea is nigh:
I fancy that its music comes
    Between the triply-breasted ships,
        Where Dublin quay clasps close the tide,
        Palace and hovel reared beside,
    And the salt wind upon my lips.

Dear City of the days long dead,
    Where hopeless Hope o'erlooks the seas,
Thy very life with Death is wed –
    Where are thy dazzling pageantries?
Where is the pride that nerved thee once –
    The glory of secure renown?
        Thou seated here, provincialised,
        Beggared and utterly despised –
    Queen with rent robe and shattered crown.

The beauty of the sunrise smites,
    With fire of heaven, thy temple walls;
The splendour of the sunset lights
    The pillared porches of thy halls;
Glory, and grace, and colour fill
    Thy measure to its wide extent;
        But thou art torpid as the kings
        Who sleep in the imprisoning rings,
    That make their grave and monument.

What man could know and love thee not,
    Even in the garments of thy shame –
Even in thy bitter, bitter lot –
    Thou stainless lady, free from blame?
Thy very pavements ring with song,
    For there the Irish heart took voice –
        There struck the high heroic chord –
        There uttered the inspiring word
    That bade the Celtic world rejoice.

If ashes be thy meed today,
    The Crown awaits thee with the Cross,
And heaven, that is thy hope and stay,
    Keeps record of each tear and loss.
The nations totter in the dust,
    Their might, their power, as shadows flee,
        But thou keep'st in those earnest eyes,
        Blue as thy radiant, sapphire skies,
    The Springtide of Eternity.

When John Francis O'Donnell (1837–1874) wrote this meditation on Dublin, he was living in Victorian London. The poem recalls the proud days before 1800, before pessimism descended on the city with the closure of the Irish Parliament House in College Green. Only faith, and the future, could ever redress the balance.

O'Donnell's short life was not a particularly merry one. An all-purpose literary journeyman, he spent much of his time in economic exile in London, getting several magazine articles and poems into *All the Year Round*, edited by Charles Dickens. Other work appeared in a baffling confusion of ephemeral journals, sometimes under the pseudonym 'Caviare' (a delicacy which can't have been a very regular part of his diet). Aware of what sort of thing each periodical was likely to pay for, he would reserve for the English papers his more delicate poems and his verses of nostalgic exile (like the one above), while his line in militantly patriotic verses was fed to the Irish papers. In the eyes of posterity, this did not do him much good in either country, though it helped to pay the landlady.

By the beginning of the twentieth century, O'Donnell (or rather, his reputation) had been rudely elbowed off the literary stage by a new wave of writers (loosely called the 'Celtic Twilight' or the 'Irish Literary Revival'), who redefined what it was to be a genuine Irish writer. At first it had seemed that his name might endure, since in 1891 the first fruit of the London-based Irish Literary Society was an edition of his poems. However, when W. B. Yeats, annoyed that the society had excluded him from its publication committee, gave his opinion that J. F. O'Donnell was not much better than a journalist, that was more or less that. Though he still has a handful of devotees, it is symptomatic that no mention of him is to be found in the 800-page *Macmillan Dictionary of Irish Literature* (1979).

Finnegan's Wake

Tim Finnegan lived in Walkin Street,
 A gentleman Irish mighty odd,
He had a tongue both rich and sweet,
 And to rise in the world he carried a hod.
Now Tim had a sort of a tippling way,
 With the love of the liquor he was born,
And to help him on with his work each day,
 He'd a drop of the craythur ev'ry morn.

Whack fol the dah, dance to your partner,
    Welt the flure, yer trotters shake,
Wasn't it the truth I told you,
    Lots of fun at Finnegan's Wake.

One morning Tim was rather full,
    His head felt heavy which made him shake,
He fell from the ladder and broke his skull,
    So they carried him home his corpse to wake.
They rolled him up in a nice clean sheet,
    And laid him out upon the bed,
With a gallon of whiskey at his feet,
    And a barrel of porter at his head.

His friends assembled at the wake,
    And Mrs Finnegan called for lunch,
First they brought in tay and cake,
    Then pipes, tobacco, and whiskey punch.
Miss Biddy O'Brien began to cry,
    'Such a neat clean corpse, did you ever see,
Arrah, Tim avourneen, why did you die?'
    'Ah, hould your gab,' said Paddy McGee.

Then Biddy O'Connor took up the job,
    'Biddy,' says she, 'you're wrong, I'm sure,'
But Biddy gave her a belt in the gob,
    And left her sprawling on the floor;
Oh, then the mighty war did rage;
    'Twas woman to woman and man to man,
Shillelagh law did all engage,
    And a row and a ruction soon began.

Then Micky Maloney raised his head,
>   When a naggin of whiskey flew at him,
It missed and falling on the bed,
>   The liquor scattered over Tim;
Bedad he revives, see how he rises,
>   And Timothy rising from the bed,
Says, 'Whirl your liquor round like blazes,
>   Thanam o'n dhoul, do ye think I'm dead?'

Henry Shaw's *Dublin Pictorial Guide and Directory of 1850*, which lists the city's more prosperous residents and traders, shows nobody with the name of Finnegan. Presumably all of them were too poor, for six decades later, the Dublin census for 1911 recorded 246 Finnegans – and 97 Finnigans – from every level of income. (Incidentally, not a single one is called Timothy.) Likewise, though Kilkenny boasts a 'Walkin Street', there isn't one in Dublin – or are the words a garbled version of 'Watling Street', a thoroughfare running down to the river near St James's Gate Brewery, which in 1850 was full of skinners and tanners? For an obsessed researcher to find the original Tim Finnegan living – and dying – in mid-nineteenth-century Dublin would appear to be quite a challenge.

Far more rewarding is the theory that this anonymous comic song came to Ireland from America, one of many stage-Irish ditties intended to cheer up the throngs of Irish immigrants who fetched up there in the nineteenth century. It may even be that 'Walkin Street' is really 'Walker Street' in New York. But who can say? The sensible approach is surely to follow the lead of James Joyce, who in 1939 named his last novel after the song, and seems neither to have known nor cared where it came from, or how authentic it was. He chose 'Finnegan's Wake' because it is a jolly, lively party piece that sounds even better after a proper feed of drink. And ever since then, it has been a Dublin song.

FROM *Oh! Bay of Dublin*

Lady Dufferin

Oh! Bay of Dublin, my heart you're troublin',
    Your beauty haunts me like a fevered dream,
Like frozen fountains that the sun sets bubbling,
    My heart's blood warms when I but hear your name;
And never till this life pulse ceases,
    My earliest thought you'll cease to be;
Oh! there's no one here knows how fair that place is,
    And no one cares how dear it is to me . . .

And at this point the author goes on to be equally enthusiastic about the mountains of Wicklow . . .

Running through the veins of Helen Selina Blackwood, Lady Dufferin (1807–67), there was blue ink by the pint. She was a granddaughter of Ireland's greatest playwright before Oscar Wilde, Richard Brinsley Sheridan, whose grandfather in turn had been the poet and punster Thomas Sheridan, friend and willing comic butt of Jonathan Swift. Her sister was Caroline Norton, author of 'The Arab's Farewell to his Steed', recited in a million Victorian drawing-rooms, while her son Frederick, Marquis of Dufferin and Ava, wrote a famous account of his trip to Iceland, *Letters from High Latitudes* (1859). More than forty years after Lord Dufferin, her first husband, expired on a ship off Belfast after an overdose of morphine, she married her frequently refused but patient suitor, a man who claimed to be the Earl of Gifford: the following month, happy at last, he died.

Almost nobody reads Lady Dufferin nowadays, neither the hideously sentimental ballad called 'The Irish Emigrant', which was her most famous poem, nor her acclaimed essay on 'Keys';

and even though the liveliest of her works, the 1863 *Lispings from Low Latitudes: Extracts from the Journals of the Hon. Impulsia Gushington*, was reprinted not long ago, few people bothered much with it then either.

After Reading J. T. Gilbert's 'History of Dublin'
Denis Florence MacCarthy

Long have I loved the beauty of thy streets,
    Fair Dublin: long, with unavailing vows,
    Sigh'd to all guardian deities who rouse
The spirits of dead nations to new heats
Of life and triumph: – vain the fond conceits,
    Nestling like eaves-warmed doves 'neath patriot brows!
    Vain as the 'Hope', that from thy Custom-House
Looks o'er the vacant bay in vain for fleets.
    Genius alone brings back the days of yore:
Look! look, what life is in these quaint old shops –
The loneliest lanes are rattling with the roar
    Of coach and chair; fans, feathers, flambeaus, fops,
Flutter and flicker through yon open door,
    Where Handel's hand moves the great organ stops.

Once upon a time the middle name of Denis Florence MacCarthy (1817–82) was not as unusual in men as it is today, though in rural parts of Ireland you may still be lucky enough to encounter a male Florence. This particular one published his first poems in the *Nation*, alongside the best work of that other three-named poet, James Clarence Mangan. In his book *Poets and Dramatists* (1846), MacCarthy nationalistically reclaimed for Ireland large numbers of nominally English writers: was it partly for this revolutionary act that he was appointed Professor of English in the new Catholic University of Ireland when it opened its doors in 1854?

That was also the year in which Volume I of John T. Gilbert's *History of the City of Dublin* appeared, the first decent account of the capital. MacCarthy read on page 75 of how in 1741 George Frederick Handel came to Dublin to conduct the première of his greatest work, the *Messiah*, and he was inspired to write the sonnet above (which is dated March 1856). The poem is graphic evidence of how, suddenly, citizens could be proud of the city as the embodiment and culmination of Ireland's rich and varied past.

The central dome of the present, reconstructed Custom House, on the north bank of the Liffey, bears a statue by Thomas Banks that 'looks o'er the vacant bay in vain for fleets': though it represents not 'Hope' but 'Commerce', perhaps it could be argued that in terms of the city's future they came to the same thing in the end. The statue, incidentally, has made a previous fleeting appearance in these pages, in J. F. O'Donnell's 'The Return'.

Dublin Jack of All Trades

I am a roving sporting blade, they call me Jack of All Trades,
I always placed my chief delight in courting pretty fair maids,
For when in Dublin I arrived to try for a situation,
I always heard them say it was the pride of all the nations.

CHORUS

I'm roving Jack of All Trades, of every trade, of all trades,
And if you wish to know my name, they call me Jack of All
  Trades.

On George's Quay I first began and there became a porter,
Me and my master soon fell out which cut my acquaintance
    shorter.
In Sackville-street a pastry cook – in James's-street a baker,
In dirty Cook-street I did coffins make, in Eustace-street a
    preacher.

In Baggot-street I drove a cab and there was well requited,
In Francis-street had lodging beds to entertain all strangers.
For Dublin is of high renown or I am much mistaken,
In Kevin-street I do declare sold butter, eggs and bacon.

In Golden Lane I sold old shoes – in Meath-street was a
    grinder,
In Barrack-street I lost my wife – I'm glad I ne'er could find her,
In Mary's Lane I've dyed old clothes of which I've often
    boasted,
In that noted place Exchequer-street sold mutton ready roasted.

In Temple Bar I dressed old hats, in Thomas-street a sawyer,
In Pill Lane I sold the plate – in Green-street an honest lawyer.
In Plunkett-street I sold cast clothes – in Bride's alley a broker,
In Charles-street I had a shop, sold shovel, tongs and poker.

In College Green a banker was – in Smithfield a drover,
In Britain-street a waiter – in George's-street a glover;
On Ormond Quay I sold old books – in King-street a nailer,
In Townsend-street a carpenter and in Rings End a sailor.

In Cole's Lane a jobbing butcher – in Dame-street a tailor,
In Moor-street a chandler and on the Coombe a weaver:
In Church-street I sold old ropes – on Redmond's hill a draper,
In Mary-street sold 'baca pipes – in Bishop-street a Quaker.

In Peter-street I was a quack – in Green-street a grazier,
On the harbour I did carry sacks, in Werburgh-street a glazier,
In Mud Island was a dairy boy where I became a scooper,
In Capel-street a barber's clerk – in Abbey-street a cooper.

In Liffey-street had furniture with fleas and bugs I sold it,
And at the bank a big placard I often stood to hold it;
In New-street I sold hay and straw and in Spitalfields made
    bacon,
In Fishamble-street was at the grand old trade of basket
    making.

In Summer Hill a coach maker, in Denzille-street a gilder,
In Clare-street a tanner – in Brunswick-street a builder;
In High-street I sold hosiery, in Patrick-street sold all blades,
So if you wish to know my name they call me Jack of all Trades.

'Dublin Jack of All Trades' has been perennially popular since
the beginning. Almost a gazetteer of the industries of Victorian
Dublin, the ballad brings its audience on a business tour of a city
pullulating with activity. The words appeared on various penny
broadsheets during the latter half of the nineteenth century, the
earliest known of which was issued in or about 1861 by John
F. Nugent and Co., a Dublin printer operating from an old
bookbindery at 35 New Row West in the Liberties. They were
probably first written down not long before this printing, for
although a seventeenth-century songsheet called 'Jolly Iack of
all Trades: OR, The Cries of London City' was in the collection of
the diarist Samuel Pepys, apart from the title neither this, nor
any other early song, shows much similarity to the Dublin one.

    This is not to say that other versions do not exist: they do;
and you can come across 'Jacks of All Trades' hailing from
London, Birmingham, Nottingham, Liverpool, Coventry and

even the English West Midlands. However, unless further evidence emerges, we hereby claim this one as the inspiration for all the rest.

Probably the most familiar – and the best – modern rendition is the one sung by the gravel-voiced Ronnie Drew of 'The Dubliners'.

Requiescat

Oscar Wilde

Tread lightly, she is near
    Under the snow,
Speak gently, she can hear
    The daisies grow.

All her bright golden hair
    Tarnished with rust,
She that was young and fair
    Fallen to dust.

Lily-like, white as snow,
    She hardly knew
She was a woman, so
    Sweetly she grew.

Coffin-board, heavy stone,
    Lie on her breast,
I vex my heart alone,
    She is at rest.

Peace, Peace, she cannot hear
    Lyre or sonnet,
All my life's buried here,
    Heap earth upon it.

Oscar Wilde (1854–1900) told W. B. Yeats, who wanted it for an anthology, that he didn't think 'Requiescat' very typical of his work. 'Still, I am glad you like it.' Typical or not, the elegy, written in memory of his eight-year-old sister Isola who died of a fever when Oscar was twelve, has remained one of his more admired poems.

While an undergraduate at TCD, Wilde would occasionally lure friends back to the family home not far away in Merrion Square, telling them that he and his mother had founded a society for the suppression of virtue. It would be charitable to call the Wilde parents eccentric – his mother was the nationalist poetess Speranza, a colossal, histrionic woman who appears rarely to have told the truth, while his comparatively diminutive father, eminent antiquarian and Surgeon-Oculist to Queen Victoria, was almost as famous for his grubby appearance and grubbier morals. He inspired a Dublin riddle that is said to have appealed to Yeats, of all people:

'Why are Sir William Wilde's nails black?'
'Because he scratches himself.'

Home life in these circumstances could only have been stressful for a sensitive and artistic young man like Oscar Wilde, and it must have been a relief when he won a scholarship to Magdalen College. 'My dear Oscar,' remarked his tutor Mahaffy, 'you are not clever enough for us in Dublin. You had better run over to Oxford.'

'Requiescat' remained unpublished until 1881, when one critic objected that golden hair does *not* go rusty in the grave. More appreciatively, a sculptor sent its author a memorial plaque depicting a young girl, which he had made to illustrate the poem. After his marriage, Wilde hung it over the mantelpiece in one of the glittering drawing-rooms of his 'House Beautiful' in Chelsea.

The doctor who had attended Isola during her last illness would remember the young Oscar as 'an affectionate, gentle, retiring, dreamy boy': the grown man was never quite to lose those characteristics. After his death in a Paris hotel room, an envelope was found among his scanty belongings. It was decorated with crosses and quotations from the Bible, and beneath the linked letters 'O' and 'I', it bore, in a boyish hand, the words 'My Isola's Hair'.

Magazine Fort, Phoenix Park
William Wilkins

Inside its zigzag lines the little camp is asleep,
    Embalm'd in the infinite breath of the greensward,
           the river, the stars.
Round the staff the yellow leopards of England,
           weary of wars,
Curl and uncurl, to the murmurous voice of the
           greenwood deep.
On the lonely terrace their watch the shadowy
           sentinels keep,
Each bayonet a spire of silver – high over the
           silvery jars
Of the streamtide, swooning in starlight adown
           its foam-fretted bars
To the city, that lies in a shroud as of ashes under
           the steep.
To the south are the hills everlasting; eastward,
           the sea-capes and isles;
Inland, the levels of emerald stretch for a
           hundred miles.

William Wilkins (1852–1915) is as obscure a poet as ever you will find, but his exquisite little poem about the old Magazine Fort deserves to be better known. It comes from the 1881 issue of an anthology of writings put out by Trinity College, Dublin, called *Kottabos* – which also published early work by Oscar Wilde. A year later, after Walt Whitman had met Oscar (and plied him with elderberry wine and milk punch), a letter arrived from a Dublin friend, Thomas W. Rolleston, who had known both Wilkins and Wilde from their Trinity days. Wilde's verse, Rolleston informed the great American poet, was 'dead and artificial – not even good singing', whereas 'a page of [Wilkins] is worth all Oscar Wilde's poetry put together'.

Unfortunately, unlike Oscar, Wilkins did not keep it up – after *Songs of Study* (1881) there were to be no more books of verse; indeed he produced very little else apart from some prose and verse for a publication uninspiringly entitled *Froth*. Perhaps, however, his influence may have had some small effect on Irish poetry after all, for he was to spend almost thirty busy years as headmaster of the High School, then in Harcourt Street – where among his pupils was a schoolboy called Willie Yeats. One thing is certain, however: even if William Wilkins taught Yeats anything about poetry, he never managed to teach him how to spell.

Cockles and Mussels

James Yorkston

In Dublin's fair city,
Where the girls are so pretty,
  I first set my eyes on sweet Molly Malone.
She wheel'd her wheelbarrow
Through streets broad and narrow,
    Crying cockles and mussels, alive, alive, o!
      Alive, alive, o! alive, alive, o!
Crying cockles and mussels, alive, alive, o!

She was a fishmonger,
But sure 'twas no wonder,
  For so were her father and mother before.
And they each wheeled their barrow
Through streets broad and narrow,
    Crying cockles and mussels, alive, alive, o!
      Alive, alive, o! *etc.*

She died of a fever,
And no one could save her,
  And that was the end of sweet Molly Malone.
But her ghost wheels the barrow,
Through streets broad and narrow,
    Crying cockles and mussels, alive, alive, o!
      Alive, alive, o!' *etc.*

Apart from mentioning Dublin in the first line, 'Cockles and Mussels' has no proven Irish credentials at all, and may have as little to do with the city as 'It's a Long Way to Tipperary' has to do with Tipperary. In fact, far from being an Irish lament, this 'traditional Irish Georgian street-ballad' is a comic burlesque from the late-Victorian music-hall, and was probably first performed in tones of the deepest tragedy, complete with mock tears and much handkerchief-work. It has been traced back no further than the 1880s, when it seems to have been issued in Edinburgh by Ernest Köhler, publisher of songbooks and music scores (and vendor of violins and other musical instruments). A certain Edward Forman is credited with 'arranging' the music, but the words were composed by James Yorkston, who by all accounts was not even Irish, but a Scot.

But no matter. With its lilting tune and a rousing chorus that dares audiences not to join in, the song is now firmly part of Dublin's folklore. In recent decades cultural historians have floated various complex speculations about Molly Malone's real identity, the nature of the fever that killed her, the date of her death and the whereabouts of her body. Some have even had the gall to suggest that she may have been offering male passers-by something considerably more spicy than shellfish.

In 1988, as part of the official celebrations for a putative one thousand years of Dublin history, a new statue representing a seventeenth-century Molly was unveiled in Grafton Street. This alluring figure, wheeling a laden handcart in the direction of Trinity College, was immediately supplied with a new name, 'the tart with the cart'. She is still there today, in her 'low-and-behold' dress that is quite unsuitable for someone with a vocation in the wet-fish trade.

With all this decidedly dubious attention, the ballad has currently fallen out of favour at home – though anyone lucky enough to hear the late Frank Harte's version, in which he delivers the words of the title as a full-throated street-cry of the sort heard in Dublin until not long ago, will surely succumb to the charms of poor Molly Malone and her memorable end.

Belts

Rudyard Kipling

There was a row in Silver Street that's near to Dublin Quay,
Between an Irish regiment an' English cavalree;
It started at Revelly an' it lasted on till dark:
The first man dropped at Harrison's, the last forninst the Park.
For it was: – 'Belts, belts, belts, an' that's one for you!'
An' it was, 'Belts, belts, belts, an' that's done for you!'
O buckle an' tongue
Was the song that we sung
From Harrison's down to the Park!

There was a row in Silver Street – the regiments was out,
They called us 'Delhi Rebels', an' we answered, 'Threes about!'
That drew them like a hornets' nest – we met them good an' large,
The English at the double an' the Irish at the charge.
Then it was: – 'Belts . . .

There was a row in Silver Street – an' I was in it too;
We passed the time o' day, an' then the belts went whirraru!
I misremember what occurred, but subsequint the storm
A *Freeman's Journal Supplemint* was all *my* uniform.
O it was: – 'Belts . . .

There was a row in Silver Street – they sent the Polis there,
The English were too drunk to know, the Irish didn't care;
But when they grew impertinint we simultaneous rose,
Till half o' them was Liffey mud an' half was tatthered clo'es.
For it was: – 'Belts . . .

There was a row in Silver Street – it might ha' raged till now,
But someone drew his side-arm clear, an' nobody knew how;
'Twas Hogan took the point an' dropped; we saw the
                                        red blood run:
An' so we all was murderers that started out in fun.
        While it was: – 'Belts . . .

There was a row in Silver Street – but that put down the shine,
Wid each man whisperin' to his next: "Twas never work o' mine!'
We went away like beaten dogs, an' down the street we bore him,
The poor dumb corpse that couldn't tell the bhoys were
                                        sorry for him.
        When it was: – 'Belts . . .

There was a row in Silver Street – it isn't over yet,
For half of us are under guard wid punishments to get;
'Tis all a merricle to me as in the Clink I lie:
There was a row in Silver Street – begod, I wonder why!
        But it was: – 'Belts, belts, belts, an' that's one for you!'
        An' it was, 'Belts, belts, belts, an' that's done for you!'
        O buckle an' tongue
        Was the song that we sung
        From Harrison's down to the Park!

This poem appeared in Kipling's *Barrack Room Ballads* in 1892.
Though he did not visit Dublin until 1911, he had been friendly
in India with Lord Roberts, Commander-in-Chief of the British
forces there, and the military Irishman may be the ultimate
source of information about the incident. Apart from 'Dublin
Quay', which should be Ellis Quay, Kipling seems to have taken
pains to get his place-names right: Silver Street, long since
renamed Ellis Street, runs north from the Liffey to Benburb

Street, near the entrance to the Royal Barracks (now Collins Barracks). In the chorus, the 'Park' is of course the Phoenix Park, its main entrance not far to the west – and could 'Harrisons', presumably a pub, possibly be the James Harrison of 22 Queen Street, just around the corner?

Like most Victorians (including many Irish Victorians), Rudyard Kipling (1865–1936) fully subscribed to the myth of the 'Fighting Irish'. Though emphatically not Irish himself, he enjoyed trying his hand at Hibernian verses, spelling out the 'brogue' in the convention of the time, now much despised. And an odd convention it was: note for instance the awkward 'forninst' (meaning 'in front of') in the first verse – and what can be the difference between the 'bhoys' of the second-last verse above and the 'boys' of standard English?

There were other English perpetrators of poems in brogue, notably W. M. Thackeray and Lord Tennyson – the latter's effort, 'Tomorrow', for example, needs to be seen to be believed. Written entirely seriously, it is tragic in more ways than one. Here is the first verse:

FROM *Tomorrow*

Alfred, Lord Tennyson

Her, that yer Honour was spakin' to? Whin, yer Honour?
                              last year –
Standin' here be the bridge, when last yer Honour
                              was here?
An' yer Honour ye gev her the top of the mornin'.
                              'Tomorra,' says she.
What did they call her, yer Honour? They call'd her
                              Molly Magee.

70

An' yer Honour's the thrue ould blood that always
                              manes to be kind,
But there's rason in all things, yer Honour, for Molly
                              was out of her mind.

In this case you might think that Molly Magee was not the only
one to be unhinged.

The Wreck of the *Vartry*

It was the good ship *Vartry*
    That sailed the sweet Liffee,
And the Skipper had taken the casks aboard,
    A goodly companee.

Blue were the labels, an azure blue
    Proclaiming Double X,
But nayther the Skipper nor the crew
    Had dreamt of storms or wrecks.

Now as she steam'd by the Ha'penny Bridge,
    The engine raised a row,
While a cloud no bigger than a midge
    Loomed up on the Starboard bow.

And as they steered by Aston's Quay,
    The look-out man grew pale,
'I feared we'd not escape,' says he,
    'MacBirney's Summer Sale!'

And ere they reached the Customs House,
    Down in a wild vortex,
The *Vartry* plunged, the cause was plain,
    She'd too much Double X.

All ye who drink of James's Gate,
  (No matter what your sex),
Take warning by the *Vartry*'s fate,
  Thro' too much Double X!

Penned by an anonymous hand this disgraceful parody of 'The Wreck of the Hesperus', Longfellow's melodramatic recitation-piece, appeared in a now forgotten Dublin comic magazine called the *Leprecaun*, probably not long after an incident on the Liffey in 1905 in which the *Vartry* somehow contrived to get into difficulties.

There were once over a dozen of these Guinness barges, liquidly christened with the names of Irish rivers. Until the early 1960s, if you peered over any of the city bridges, you might have seen one steaming downstream to the quay in front of the Customs House, loaded with barrels from the brewery at St James's Gate. If Dublin lore is to be trusted (which it rarely is), the wheelmen, as they lowered their smokestacks to squeeze under O'Connell Bridge, must have grown heartily sick of requests shouted down by urchins to 'Bring us back a parrot!'

The *Vartry*, built in 1902, was a substantial craft, with a length of almost eighty feet, so if it did actually sink, it can't have been easy to refloat. After the brewery gave up using the vessels, it saw service in the Ulster clay trade on Lough Neagh, where her remains can still be seen half-submerged near Toomebridge. A plan to bring her back to life for a third time, as a tourist craft on the Liffey, has not yet materialised.

The barges carried barrels filled with two different types of Guinness: 'Double X' stout (the familiar draught Guinness of today), and the cheaper – and less alcoholic – 'Single X' porter, which is no longer produced. Porter, also known as 'plain', was the one celebrated in 'A Pint of Plain is Your Only Man', Flann O'Brien's famous 'pome' in *At Swim-Two-Birds*.

On an Anniversary

[AFTER READING THE DATES IN A BOOK OF LYRICS]

John Millington Synge

> With Fifteen-ninety or Sixteen-sixteen
> We end Cervantes, Marot, Nashe or Green:
> Then Sixteen-thirteen till two score and nine,
> Is Crashaw's niche, that honey-lipped divine.
> And so when all my little work is done
> They'll say I came in Eighteen-seventy-one,
> And died in Dublin . . . What year will they write
> For my poor passage to the stall of night?

John M. Synge (1871–1909) did die in Dublin, not very long after writing this gloomy prophecy. W. B. Yeats admired and even loved 'that meditative man', and so did Jack, his painter brother, who summed up in a memorial volume what the playwright had meant to him:

> If he had lived in the days of piracy he would have been fiddler in a pirate-schooner, him they called 'the music'. 'The music' looked on at everything with dancing eyes but drew no sword, and when the schooner was taken and the pirates hung at Cape Corso Castle or the Island of Saint Christopher's, 'the music' was spared because he *was* 'the music'.

Synge's reputation continues to grow, despite a persistent strand of opinion in Ireland that the stylised language of his plays is grossly patronising. Flann O'Brien, writing in the *Irish Times* as Myles na gCopaleen, once caustically accused Synge, or rather his shade, of presenting 'amusing clowns talking a sub-language of their own'. It was all very well in the old days, he observed, when we in Ireland kept Synge and his like to

73

ourselves, but 'words choke in the pen when one comes to describe what happened to us when the English discovered that we were rawther interesting peepul ek'tully, that we were nice, witty, brave, fearfully seltic and fiery, lovable, strong, boozy, impulsive, hospitable, decent and so on till you weaken'.

Posterity treats many fine poets and artists so badly that it can hardly be the great judge that it is always cracked up to be, but in this case it has – so far – come down firmly on the side of Synge.

Nelson Street

Seumas O'Sullivan

There is hardly a mouthful of air
In the room where the breakfast is set,
For the blind is still down though it's late,
And the curtains are redolent yet
Of tobacco smoke, stale from last night.
There's the little bronze teapot, and there
The eggs on the blue willow-plate,
And the sleepy canary, a hen,
Starts faintly her chirruping tweet
And I know, could she speak, she would say,
'Hullo there – what's wrong with the light,
Draw the blind up, let's look at the day.'
I see that it's Monday again,
For the man with the organ is there;
Every Monday he comes to the street
(Lest I, or the bird there, should miss
Our count of monotonous days)
With his reed-organ, wheezy and sweet,
And stands by the window and plays
'There's a Land that is Fairer than This'.

Seumas O'Sullivan (1879–1958), whose real name was James Starkey, was at his happiest when browsing the bookstalls along the Liffey quays. An all-round literary man, he found his voice in atmospheric vignettes of life in Dublin's crumbling Georgian streets and squares. Later, he became an evocative essayist and writer of gentlemanly memoirs, and as editor of the *Dublin Magazine* he published the early work of two generations of Irish writers. He is said once to have turned down a poem by Samuel Beckett because he was uncertain whether it was obscene or not, but then discovered that nobody else he showed it to could tell either.

In 1909, when the lines above appeared, Nelson Street was in a modestly genteel residential area on the north side of the city. It lies at right angles to Eccles Street, where Joyce placed Leopold Bloom's (fictional) house in *Ulysses*.

Asquith in Dublin

Thomas Kettle

You stopped your steps, and the music marched, and
                        the torches tossed
As you filled your streets with your comic Pentecost,
And the little English went by and the lights grew dim;
We, dumb in the shouting crowd, we thought of him.

Of him, too great for our souls and ways,
Too great for our laughter or love, praise or dispraise,
Of him, and the wintry swords, and the closing gloom –
Of him going forth alone to his lonely doom.

No shouts, my Dublin then! Not a light nor a cry –
You kept them all till now, when the little English go by!

Economist, lawyer, poet, champion of women's suffrage, MP for East Tyrone and native Dubliner, Thomas Kettle (1880–1916) had an orator's gift for words: in a speech to the House of Commons in 1910, he summed up Rudyard Kipling as 'formerly a poet and now a contributor to the *Daily Telegraph*'.

'Asquith in Dublin' is an angry poem: Kettle scribbled it down in August 1912, when, with legislation imminent that pledged to grant Home Rule to Ireland at last, the visiting British Prime Minister paraded through the streets to a tumultuous welcome. Sickened by Dublin's toadying gratitude for being offered what morally already belonged to them, Kettle recalls how, a generation before, Ireland had turned its back on the real father of the Home Rule Bill, Charles Stuart Parnell. In 1890, traduced by the English, vilified by the Roman Catholic Church and abandoned by his supporters, Parnell had left Ireland a broken man, and 'gone to his lonely doom', dying in Brighton within a year. (Many Dubliners would disagree with Kettle's attitude – the point is often made that the capital was the one part of the island that retained a commitment to 'The Chief'.)

To be, as Kettle was, an urbane peace-loving Irish nationalist was a rare enough combination. It would lead him to see the 1916 Easter Rising as a foolish and unnecessary exercise: after all, the British *had* promised Home Rule the moment the First World War was over. In October of that year he was killed on the Somme, fighting against Germany for the cause of 'a free united Ireland in a free Europe'. After his death, the Irish light essayist Robert Lynd, who had known him, wrote that Kettle had 'meditated on goals rather than marched to them'. As an epitaph, it was grossly unjust.

FROM *Átha Cliath*

'An Gam Eile'

I read Walt Whitman's 'Mannahatta'
And I thought, 'What can I say about my city?'
I looked first to the meaning of its name, Átha Cliath, the Ford
    of the Hurdles,
And then to the name Dubh linn;
Neither gave me any inspiration,
We have missed the Ford of the Hurdles
And we do not call it Dubh linn but Dublin –
Still I thought, 'What can I say about my city?'
And I thought, 'I will say everything about it.'
Like St Paul, I am a citizen of no mean city,
Though I have not got a vote for municipal elections;
I do not want a vote until I can see some use to put it to.
And I can see no use for it at present;
None the less, I am very proud of my citizenship,
Which is a thing independent of the franchise
And infinitely more precious.
My city is a very old city,
Though not an ancient city in the archaeological sense;
Some say it was founded by the Danes, that is, the Norsemen
    of the race of Sigerson, in the ninth century,
But I have read in a translation of a sixth-century tradition of a
    town called Átha Cliath,
And I believe that there was always a town where the Liffey
    flows into the bay,
Unless my ancestors were greater fools than I think them.
But it was the Norsemen made my city a strong place and a
    fortification,

And consequently a nucleus to be coveted by subsequent
    would-be conquerors,
And it was the Norsemen who developed the commerce of the
    Port of Dublin,
Setting a mercenary example to the modern town of Belfast,
And thus laying the foundations of the British Empire,
Which to you and me is known as the Empire of Death.
Whoever it was built the Castle of Dublin,
Is assuredly built into the Castle of Hell.
The idea of the City Castle is hateful
As it is hateful to be dominant and domineering,
And still more hateful to be predominant.
Dublin was never predominant in Ireland,
Though it has long been the chief city;
It has never been a capital in the same sense that London is a
    capital,
A place upon which the whole country is economically
    dependent for supply and demand:
Supply of governing capacity and control units,
And aristocrats and snobs and Jews and money;
And demand for lives and labour and virtue to be perverted,
    and food and drink and vice. [. . .]
But Dublin is the capital in the sense of being the chief city
And the *Arbiter elegantiarum* for the whole of the United
    Kingdom
Of Ulster, Munster, Leinster, Connaught and Meath.
And when they become conscious of their deficiencies in
    England they look to us also.
If you were to take London with an army, you would destroy
    the British Empire;
If you were to take Paris, France would have to make terms;

But if you were to take Dublin, Rathmines would go on
    fighting,
And maybe send you back with a flea in your ear. [. . .]
I left Dublin in order to come back to it,
For whereas I used to live in Dublin, now I live in Donnybrook
    – and go to town every day, or nearly every day;
I might go oftener if the trams were more democratic,
But sometimes I almost stifle in their snobbish atmosphere,
And a penny is a lot of money to spend all at once, unless on a
    joy ride with your best girl, and that would be at least
    twopence,
And would be well worth it.

'Baile Átha Cliath', literally, 'the Town of the Hurdle Ford', is the
usual name for Dublin in the Irish language. The lines above were
found in the June 1914 issue of *National Student*, the under-
graduate magazine of University College, Dublin. The poem (if
poem it be) begins as a parody of Walt Whitman's shout of joy for
his native New York, 'Mannahatta', from his *Leaves of Grass* – a
collection that in certain Irish circles was thought dangerously
ultramodern, even though it dated back to the 1850s.

As our anonymous author warms to his task, he extends his
remit far beyond Whitman's original. We are given a vivid
portrait of the philosophical, social and political confusion that
reigned in the capital in the years just before the Easter Rising.
And then, at the end of the poem, just to avoid any embarrassing
misunderstandings, 'An Gam Eile' (in Irish, 'The Other Idiot')
makes it absolutely clear that whatever people might say about
Walt Whitman's predilections, he was very keen on women
himself.

A Dublin Ballad – 1916

'Dermot O'Byrne'

O write it up above your hearth
And troll it out to sun and moon,
To all true Irishmen on earth
Arrest and death come late or soon.

Some boy-o whistled *Ninety-eight*
One Sunday night in College Green,
And such a broth of love and hate
Was stirred ere Monday morn was late
As Dublin town had never seen.

And god-like forces shocked and shook
Through Irish hearts that lively day,
And hope it seemed no ill could brook.
Christ! for that liberty they took
There was the ancient deuce to pay!

The deuce in all his bravery,
His girth and gall grown no whit less,
He swarmed in from the fatal sea
With pomp of huge artillery
And brass and copper haughtiness.

He cracked up all the town with guns
That roared loud psalms to fire and death,
And houses hailed down granite tons
To smash our wounded underneath.

And when at last the golden bell
Of liberty was silenced – then
He learned to shoot extremely well
At unarmed Irish gentlemen!

Ah! where were Michael and gold Moll
And Seumas and my drowsy self?
Why did fate blot us from the scroll?
Why were we left upon the shelf,

Fooling with trifles in the dark
When the light struck so wild and hard?
Sure our hearts were as good a mark
For Tommies up before the lark
At rifle practice in the yard!

Well, the last fire is trodden down,
Our dead are rotting fast in lime,
We all can sneak back into town,
Stravague about as in old time,

And stare at gaps of grey and blue
Where Lower Mount Street used to be,
And where flies hum round muck we knew
For Abbey Street and Eden Quay.

And when the devil's made us wise
Each in his own peculiar hell,
With desert hearts and drunken eyes
We're free to sentimentalise
By corners where the martyrs fell.

When 'A Dublin Ballad – 1916' was first published in 1918, the British Government suppressed it as subversive. Its author, 'Dermot O'Byrne', was in reality Arnold Bax (1883–1953), a Londoner who in his early twenties fell under the spell of Yeats and all his works. In 1905 Bax had moved to Ireland, where he liked to think of himself as a true Celt – hence his use of broguish words like 'stravague' (saunter) above. He threw himself into Dublin's highly politicised literary scene, spending a good deal of time with Joseph Plunkett, Padraic Pearse and Thomas MacDonagh, young nationalist poets who in 1916 would become signatories of the Proclamation of the Irish Republic: all three were executed for their part in the Easter Rising. Though Bax never turned his back on his Irish phase, his true calling was as a composer and his true nationality English, and eventually he agreed to 'shuffle around in knee-breeches' as Master of the King's Musick, graciously accepting a knighthood from His Majesty in 1942.

A Year Ago Today

H. A. MacCartan

(An incident related to me by the proprietress of a
little County Wicklow Hotel in July 1916.)

A year ago this very day
    They came into my little place
From Dublin town, I heard them say,
    Greeting me with an old-world grace.
And though I knew not who they were
    Or what their mission, yet I knew
They did not breathe the common air
    But to some higher aim were true.

The eyes of one were mildly sad
    As though for hopes beyond recall;
A dreamer's face the second had,
    But proud and falcon-like withal;
And one was gayer than a boy
    Rejoicing in the summer's pride,
Quick to waylay each furtive joy,
    Eager to scan horizons wide.

They lingered till the day grew old;
    The hours flew by on silver wings,
With talk and mirth and songs that told
    The tale of Ireland's sorrowings.
And when they rose to say goodbye,
    And thank me in their boyish way,
I think my eyes were scarcely dry:
    I had not known so sweet a day.

Soon afterwards their names I heard –
  Plunkett, Pearse, MacDonagh – three
Poets whose ardent hearts were stirred
  By wistful dreams of Ireland free.
And when the news came they were dead,
  That they had paid the martyr's price,
Ah, bitter were the tears I shed
  At that too grievous sacrifice.

These were the chairs they sat upon,
  This is the piano Plunkett played
With girlish fingers; now they're gone
  The room seems haunted by their shade.
They gave to Ireland all they had,
  To me they gave one golden day.
And yet I am not wholly sad:
  Their souls in heavenly gardens stray.

Hugh Augustine MacCartan (1895–1943), an Ulsterman from County Down, is not one of Ireland's most familiar literary names. As a relatively young man he wrote *Little White Roads and Other Poems* (1916), closely followed by *Silhouettes: Some Character Studies from North and South*. In 1921 he produced a volume unpromisingly entitled *The Glamour of Belfast* which, a contemporary reviewer remarked, contained 'never a trace of denunciation or abuse, but always an eye for the redeeming qualities even of Orange fanatics'. This faint early promise as a writer seems to have been eclipsed by the demands of family and career, for marriage in 1922 was followed by a move to Dublin, where in the new Free State he became a Civil Servant in the Department of Agriculture. Only one more book appeared after this upheaval, *O'Neill's Folly* (1929), a novel about gun-running set in Ulster in 1913.

'A Year Ago Today' was written very soon after the execution of the leaders of the Easter Rising, and gives us a rare sighting of the young enthusiasts before they were swept away by the actions that they were planning for Dublin. The novelist and poet Katharine Tynan, in a short review in the Irish quarterly *Studies* (No. 22, June 1917), praised the 'occasional felicities' that she found in *Little White Roads*. This poem is certainly one of them.

The Irish Free State

I went to see David, to London to David,
I went to see David, and what did he do?
He gave me a Free State, a nice little Free State,
A Free State that's bound up with Red, White and Blue.

I brought it to Dublin to show to Dáil Éireann,
I brought it to Dublin, and what did they do?
They asked me what kind of a thing was a Free State,
A Free State that's tied up with Red, White and Blue?

'Three quarters of Ireland a nation,' I told them,
'Tied on to the Empire with Red, White and Blue;
And an oath they must swear to King George and
                                    Queen Mary,
An oath they must swear to the son-in-law new.'

I'm teaching them Irish and painting their boxes
All over with green, sure, what more can I do?
Yet they tell me they want just an Irish Republic
Without any trimmings of Red, White and Blue!

On 6 December 1921, the British Prime Minister, David Lloyd George, and an Irish delegation of senior Sinn Féin politicians, including Michael Collins, signed the Anglo-Irish Treaty in London. This offered, for twenty-six of the island's thirty-two counties, a Free State *within* the British Commonwealth, but left much of Ulster still a part of the United Kingdom. Back home a month later, Dáil Éireann, the Irish Parliament, narrowly ratified the treaty, but Eamon De Valera, who had sent the delegation in the first place, disagreed and walked out. It was at about this point that the anonymous song above was circulating around Dublin. It neatly sums up the ideological divide that would soon lead to a grim and inconclusive year of civil war in Ireland.

Liffey Bridge

Oliver St John Gogarty

I gazed along the waters at the West,
Watching the low sky colour into flame,
Until each narrowing steeple I could name
Grew dark as the far vapours, and my breast
With silence like a sorrow was possessed,
And men as moving shadows went and came;
The smoke that stained the sunset seemed like shame,
Or lust, or some great evil unexpressed.

Then with a longing for the taintless air,
I called that desolation back again,
Which reigned when Liffey's widening banks were bare:
Before Ben Edair gazed upon the Dane,
Before the Hurdle Ford, and long before
Fionn drowned the young men by its meadowy shore.

Although Gogarty's sonnet was first published (under the title 'O'Connell Bridge') in the October 1904 issue of the literary magazine *Dana*, when it reappeared in his 1923 collection, *An Offering of Swans*, it seemed to echo the unease that pervaded a city that so lately had been at war with itself.

But nostalgic pessimism is not the tone we normally associate with the irrepressible Oliver St John Gogarty (1878–1957). An unrivalled composer of (still quoted) filthy limericks as well as lyric verses, he was also an athlete, a surgeon, a Senator, an amateur aviator, a novelist and, naturally, yet another of Dublin's illustrious wits. It was he who remarked, for example, that the trees by the Grand Canal, under which prostitutes used to operate on rainy nights, were 'more sinned against than sinning'.

Gogarty later put many of his friends into his books, rarely bothering to disguise them, but he was never willing to forgive one of his oldest, James Joyce, for turning him into the decidedly unsympathetic 'Malachi Mulligan' in *Ulysses*. For reasons that have not been convincingly explained, Joyce used his novel to exact a cruel revenge on his one-time roommate: one can only imagine the painful beating of Gogarty's heart in 1922 as he scoured the 730 dense pages of the book's first edition, desperately trying to work out exactly what Joyce was telling the world about him.

Disillusioned, even disgusted, by De Valera's new Ireland, Gogarty moved to America in 1939. He spent his last eighteen years as something of a professional Irishman in New York, delivering occasional lectures and writing a little.

Beautiful Lofty Things

W. B. Yeats

Beautiful lofty things: O'Leary's noble head;
My father upon the Abbey stage, before him a raging
    crowd:
'This Land of Saints,' and then as the applause died out,
'Of plaster Saints'; his beautiful mischievous head thrown
    back.
Standish O'Grady supporting himself between the tables
Speaking to a drunken audience high nonsensical words;
Augusta Gregory seated at her great ormolu table,
Her eightieth winter approaching: 'Yesterday he threatened
    my life.
I told him that nightly from six to seven I sat at this table,
The blinds drawn up'; Maud Gonne at Howth station
    waiting a train,
Pallas Athene in that straight back and arrogant head.
All the Olympians; a thing never known again.

All through his long life, people noticed W. B. Yeats (1865–1939).
Perhaps most famously, the novelist George Moore noticed him at
the home of Lady Gregory, Coole Park, as he stood 'lost in
meditation before a white congregation of swans assembled on
the lake, looking himself in his old cloak like a huge umbrella left
behind by some picnic party'.

But then, Yeats always noticed people too. In his work he had
the knack of making the particulars of his life into the universal.
It would be possible to check and expand upon all the details of
the poem above by consulting the mass of surviving material –

books, papers, letters – that document his life and times: the early influence of the almost legendary Fenian, John O'Leary; his artist father, John Butler Yeats, admonishing the Abbey Theatre audience as they shouted down *The Playboy of the Western World* in 1907 ('Isn't Mr Synge the bloody old snot to write such a play?' groaned the stage carpenter); O'Grady drunk at a Trinity dinner, the lonely, grand old man of the Irish Literary Revival exhorting the sons of Ireland to fight English decadence; the poet's faithful colleague Lady Gregory defying threats from trigger-happy 'patriots'; and the proud beauty of the woman who obsessed him for decades, Maud Gonne.

The year after Yeats's death, a younger Irish poet, Louis MacNeice, in a review of *Last Poems* (which included 'Beautiful Lofty Things') described the collection as 'the Indian summer of his virile, gossipy, contumacious, arrogant, magnificently eccentric old age'. In the poems about his friends, he wrote, Yeats was once again going around 'with a highly coloured spotlight'. And why not? He had valued them far too much to be prosaic about them. As he put it in another great poem from that late flowering, 'The Municipal Gallery Revisited', 'my glory was I had such friends.'

Dicey Reilly

A SONG

Ah poor old Dicey Reilly, she has taken to the sup,
And poor old Dicey Reilly, she will never give it up.
It's off each morning to the pop then she goes in for
    another little drop,
But the heart of the rowl is Dicey Reilly.

She will walk along Fitzgibbon Street with an independent air
And then it's down by Summerhill, and as the people stare
She'll say, 'It's nearly half past one, time I went in for
    another little one,'
But the heart of the rowl is Dicey Reilly.

Now at two, pubs close and out she goes as happy as a lark,
She'll find a bench to sleep it off down in St Patrick's Park.
She'll wake at five feeling in the pink and say, ' 'Tis time for
    another drink,'
But the heart of the rowl is Dicey Reilly.

Now she'll travel far to a dockside bar to have another round
And after one or two or three she doesn't feel quite sound
And after four she's a bit unstable; after five underneath
    the table,
But the heart of the rowl is Dicey Reilly.

Oh they carry her home at twelve o'clock as they do every
    night
Bring her inside, put her on the bed and then turn out the light.
Next morning she'll get out of bed and look for a curer for
    her head,
But the heart of the rowl is Dicey Reilly.

Ah poor old Dicey Reilly, she has taken to the sup,
And poor old Dicey Reilly, she will never give it up.
It's off each morning to the pop then she goes in for another
    little drop,
But the heart of the rowl is Dicey Reilly.

As so often with anonymous ballads, this one has several variants. In the 1960s the enterprising Dominic Behan even took the song as reproduced above and (partly to secure the copyright) added some extra verses of his own. These placed poor old Dicey in the company of the illustrious May Oblong and Becky Cooper, real-life night-ladies from the Dublin 'houses of imprudence', who had already been variously portrayed by their erstwhile patrons, James Joyce and Oliver Gogarty, and by Dominic's brother Brendan.

But entertaining as these additions may be, here we must allow Dicey Reilly to keep the shreds of dignity that have sustained her so long. Since well before the glory days of Donnybrook Fair, the regular consumption of disabling quantities of alcohol was seen as a defining characteristic of the Dublin man. More than one writer made a reputation out of it. But the city's women are usually left out of the picture, because until fairly recently they were discouraged and even banned from frequenting public houses: female tippling generally took place behind closed doors. Dicey is a notable exception, and the anonymous ballad she inspired may stand as an early anthem of Women's Liberation. Dicey Reilly is truly a citizen of credit and renown as she sets off on her morning shuttle between pawnshop and pub, and she is loved: they bring her home each night. The 'heart of the rowl' is a rare compliment, being the moist centre – and therefore the best part – of a quid of plug (or chewing) tobacco.

Enueg I

Samuel Beckett

Exeo in a spasm
tired of my darling's red sputum
from the Portobello Private Nursing Home
its secret things
and toil to the crest of the surge of the steep perilous bridge
and lapse down blankly under the scream of the hoarding
round the bright stiff banner of the hoarding
into a black west
throttled with clouds.

Above the mansions the algum-trees
the mountains
my skull sullenly
clot of anger
skewered aloft strangled in the cang of the wind
bites like a dog against its chastisement.

I trundle along rapidly now on my ruined feet
flush with the livid canal;
at Parnell Bridge a dying barge
carrying a cargo of nails and timber
rocks itself softly in the foaming cloister of the lock;
on the far bank a gang of down and outs would seem to be
    mending a beam.

Then for miles only wind
and the weals creeping alongside on the water
and the world opening up to the south
across a travesty of champaign to the mountains

and the stillborn evening turning a filthy green
manuring the night fungus
and the mind annulled
wrecked in wind.

I splashed past a little wearish old man,
Democritus,
scuttling along between a crutch and a stick,
his stump caught up horribly, like a claw, under his breech,
        smoking.
Then because a field on the left went up in a sudden blaze
of shouting and urgent whistling and scarlet and blue
        ganzies
I stopped and climbed the bank to see the game.
A child fidgeting at the gate called up:
'Would we be let in Mister?'
'Certainly' I said 'you would.'
But, afraid, he set off down the road.
'Well' I called after him 'why wouldn't you go on in?'
'Oh' he said, knowingly,
'I was in that field before and I got put out.'
So on,
derelict,
as from a bush of gorse on fire in the mountain after dark,
or in Sumatra the jungle hymen,
the still flagrant rafflesia.

Next:
a lamentable family of grey verminous hens,
perishing out in the sunk field,
trembling, half asleep, against the closed door of a shed,
with no means of roosting.
The great mushy toadstool,

green-black,
oozing up after me,
soaking up the tattered sky like an ink of pestilence,
in my skull the wind going fetid,
the water . . .

Next:
on the hill down from the Fox and Geese into Chapelizod
a small malevolent goat, exiled on the road,
remotely pucking the gate of his field;
the Isolde Stores a great perturbation of sweaty heroes,
in their Sunday best,
come hastening down for a pint of nepenthe or moly or half
    and half
from watching the hurlers above in Kilmainham.

Blotches of doomed yellow in the pit of the Liffey;
the fingers of the ladders hooked over the parapet,
soliciting;
a slush of vigilant gulls in the grey spew of the sewer.

Ah the banner
the banner of meat bleeding
on the silk of the seas and the arctic flowers
that do not exist.

Samuel Beckett (1906–89) is far better known as a playwright
and novelist than as a poet. Like James Joyce a generation before,
he showed Dublin a clean pair of heels as soon as he reasonably
could. While many of their contemporaries vamoosed to Britain
or America, they both chose to live and work on the Continent,
to become Europeans. In Paris, Beckett got to know Joyce while
he was working on *Finnegans Wake*, and they were friends for a

while. Like the older man, Beckett was to visit and revisit in his writings the Dublin he had known in youth, its physical detail and its atmosphere. But there were stark differences too between the writers. They had contrasting religious backgrounds and family means; and it also mattered that Joyce was at heart a northsider, while Beckett had spent his most impressionable years in the leafy suburb of Foxrock, a long way south of the Liffey – in Dublin terms a distinction that is far more than just a topographical one.

'Eneug I' is Beckett's jaded account of a walk he took out of the city on the Grand Canal towpath and back again along the River Liffey. It was first published in his early collection, *Echo's Bones and Other Precipitates* (1935). The strange word in the poem's title is Provençal, meaning something like 'A Song of Irritation' or 'A List of Annoying Things', and is normally applied to a type of Troubador verse. One cause for the poet's exasperation on this occasion may be that Beckett wrote it while awaiting an operation on a hammer toe: the long afternoon's hike on 'ruined feet' must have been quite painful enough to inspire an *eneug*. Later, he succinctly explained to a friend why, unlike most of his poetry, 'Enueg I' still appealed to him: it had, he felt, 'something arborescent or of the sky, not Wagner, not clouds on wheels; written above an abscess and not out of a cavity, a statement and not a description of heat in the spirit to compensate for pus in the spirit.'

Dublin Made Me

Donagh MacDonagh

Dublin made me and no little town
With the country closing in on its streets,
The cattle walking proudly on its pavements,
The jobbers, the gombeenmen and the cheats

Devouring the Fair Day between them,
A public-house to half a hundred men,
And the teacher, the solicitor and the bank-clerk
In the hotel bar, drinking for ten.

Dublin made me, not the secret poteen still,
The raw and hungry hills of the West,
The lean road flung over profitless bog
Where only a snipe could nest,

Where the sea takes its tithe of every boat.
Bawneen and curragh have no allegiance of mine,
Nor the cute, self-deceiving talkers of the South
Who look to the East for a sign.

The soft and dreary midlands with their tame canals
Wallow between sea and sea, remote from adventure,
And Northward a far and fortified province
Crouches under the lash of arid censure.

I disclaim all fertile meadows, all tilled land,
The evil that grows from it, and the good,
But the Dublin of old statutes, this arrogant city,
Stirs proudly and secretly in my blood.

It can readily be appreciated that the city might stir proudly in the blood of the author of 'Dublin Made Me'. When Donagh MacDonagh (1912–68) was three, his father, the poet Thomas MacDonagh, was shot in Kilmainham Jail for his part in the Easter Rising. A year later his mother died as well, by drowning. The title is almost literally true, for after these traumas the city gave him a good education, in school and out of it, which in turn led to a successful legal, literary and gentlemanly life. This poem, which is perhaps his greatest, proves that, without compromising your patriotic credentials, you could at last openly prefer the streets of 'alien' Dublin to anywhere else on the island.

Bag-Snatching in Dublin

Stevie Smith

Sisley
Walked so nicely
With footsteps so discreet
To see her pass
You'd never guess
She walked upon the street.

Down where the Liffy waters' turgid flood
Churns up to greet the ocean-driven mud,
A bruiser in a fix
Murdered her for 6/6.

For most of her life, the impeccably English Stevie Smith (1902–71) lived with her aunt ('lion aunt', she called her) in Palmers Green, a suburb of North London. She is remembered today largely for a single, perfect, poem, 'Not Waving But Drowning'.

Despite her demure, even prim (Sisley-like) appearance, Miss Smith was always half in love with the idea of death, a trait that can be seen in her three unclassifiable novels. As for the eloquent poem here, she may misspell the River Liffey, but she is quite correct in suggesting that streetwalkers used to patrol its lower quays – though it is highly unlikely that she ever made an exploratory expedition to check. Even when this poem was written, six shillings and sixpence (less than one third of a pound) was very little to get yourself murdered for.

Dublin

Louis MacNeice

Grey brick upon brick,
Declamatory bronze
On sombre pedestals –
O'Connell, Grattan, Moore –
And the brewery tugs and the swans
On the balustraded stream
And the bare bones of a fanlight
Over a hungry door
And the air soft on the cheek
And porter running from the taps
With a head of yellow cream
And Nelson on his pillar
Watching his world collapse.

This was never my town,
I was not born nor bred
Nor schooled here and she will not
Have me alive or dead

But yet she holds my mind
With her seedy elegance,
With her gentle veils of rain
And all her ghosts that walk
And all that hide behind
Her Georgian façades –
The catcalls and the pain,
The glamour of her squalor,
The bravado of her talk.

The lights jig in the river
With a concertina movement
And the sun comes up in the morning
Like barley-sugar on the water
And the mist on the Wicklow hills
Is close, as close
As the peasantry were to the landlord,
As the Irish to the Anglo-Irish,
As the killer is close one moment
To the man he kills,
Or as the moment itself
Is close to the next moment.

She is not an Irish town
And she is not English,
Historic with guns and vermin
And the cold renown
Of a fragment of Church latin,
Of an oratorical phrase.
But oh the days are soft,
Soft enough to forget
The lesson better learnt,

The bullet on the wet
Streets, the crooked deal,
The steel behind the laugh,
The Four Courts burnt.

Fort of the Dane,
Garrison of the Saxon,
Augustan capital
Of a Gaelic nation,
Appropriating all
The alien brought,
You give me time for thought
And by a juggler's trick
You poise the toppling hour –
O greyness run to flower,
Grey stone, grey water,
And brick upon grey brick.

Louis MacNeice (1907–63) spent the majority of his adult life in England. He once defined himself as 'an Irishman of Southern blood and Northern upbringing, whose father was a Protestant Bishop and also a fervent Home Ruler'. It was a good foundation upon which to construct a poem about the contradictory city of Dublin.

MacNeice wrote it in August 1939, at the beginning of a five-month stay in Ireland, while war was about to engulf the rest of Europe. In holiday mood, he began the trip in Dublin. The neutral capital was, as he later said, 'a dance of lights in the Liffey, bacon and eggs and Guinness, laughter in the slums and salons, gossip sufficient to the day'. He climbed the spiral stair-case to the top of Nelson's Pillar (which few natives ever did), and looked out over the city. Dublin was grey, its imperial, religious and mercantile buildings were grey; its limestone and granite bridges, colleges, churches, banks, cinemas; east towards the sea, the Custom House and its quays, grey, and upriver, the Four Courts, King's Inns and the old Royal Barracks. Even the red-brick houses that lined the rotting Georgian streets were a dirty dark grey, dyed by too many years of coal smoke. And down below him in O'Connell Street, lay the great grey General Post Office, bloody heart of the Easter Rising a generation before.

Later, what people in the city most resented about his Dublin poem was the Ulsterman's proud assertion, 'she will not / Have me alive or dead'; not many knew that just days after writing these words, he had applied for the Chair of English at Trinity College. Despite a recommendation from T. S. Eliot, he was turned down. Dublin had never really wanted him anyway.

If Ever You Go to Dublin Town

Patrick Kavanagh

If ever you go to Dublin town
In a hundred years or so
Inquire for me in Baggot Street
And what I was like to know.
O he was a queer one,
Fol dol the di do,
He was a queer one
I tell you.

My great-grandmother knew him well,
He asked her to come and call
On him in his flat and she giggled at the thought
Of a young girl's lovely fall.

O he was dangerous,
Fol dol the di do,
He was dangerous
I tell you.

On Pembroke Road look out for my ghost,
Dishevelled with shoes untied,
Playing through the railings with little children
Whose children have long since died.
O he was a nice man,
Fol dol the di do,
He was a nice man
I tell you.

Go into a pub and listen well
If my voice still echoes there,
Ask the men what their grandsires thought
And tell them to answer fair.
O he was eccentric,
Fol dol the di do,
He was eccentric
I tell you.

He had the knack of making men feel
As small as they really were
Which meant as great as God had made them
But as males they disliked his air.
O he was a proud one,
Fol dol the di do,
He was a proud one
I tell you.

If ever you go to Dublin town
In a hundred years or so
Sniff for my personality,
Is it Vanity's vapour now?
O he was a vain one,
Fol dol the di do,
He was a vain one
I tell you.

I saw his name with a hundred others
In a book in the library,
It said he had never fully achieved
His potentiality.
O he was slothful,
Fol dol the di do,
He was slothful
I tell you.

He knew that posterity has no use
For anything but the soul,
The lines that speak the passionate heart,
The spirit that lives alone.
O he was a lone one,
Fol dol the di do,
Yet he lived happily
I tell you.

Patrick Kavanagh (1905–67) was born and raised on a farm in
the border county of Monaghan, but lived most of his life in
Dublin, where the spiteful called him 'The Ploughboy about
Town'. Sensitive and self-aware, he eked out a slender living
from his pen, selling his poems to magazines and newspapers,

writing two novels based on his early life, and churning out film reviews and chatty articles for anyone prepared to print them. As he grew older, alcohol and argument became his staples, and his ill-tempered battles with rival writers in public houses were proverbial. Occasionally, the fury bubbled over and solidified as satire – he had a real contempt for those who frittered away their small talents:

FROM *The Paddiad, or the Devil as a Patron of Irish Letters*

Patrick Kavanagh

> In the corner of a Dublin pub
> This party opens – blub-a-blub –
> Paddy Whiskey, Rum and Gin,
> Paddy Three sheets in the wind;
> Paddy of the Celtic Mist,
> Paddy Connemara West,
> Chestertonian Paddy Frog
> Croaking nightly in the bog.
> All the Paddies having fun
> Since Yeats handed in his gun.
> Every man completely blind
> To the truth about his mind. [. . .]

Dubliners enjoyed trying to identify which of these Paddies was which. The actor Micheál MacLiammóir, in a review in the *Sunday Times*, disapproved of 'The Paddiad', however. Patrick Kavanagh, he said, 'ought to be out on the hillside with Ariel instead of snarling in a snug with a bunch of suburban Calibans'. For all the poem's entertainment value, he was probably right.

Lines Written on a Seat on the Grand Canal, Dublin
'ERECTED TO THE MEMORY OF MRS DERMOT O'BRIEN'

Patrick Kavanagh

O commemorate me where there is water,
Canal water preferably, so stilly
Greeny at the heart of summer. Brother,
Commemorate me thus beautifully.
Where by a lock Niagariously roars
The falls for those who sit in the tremendous silence
Of mid-July. No one will speak in prose
Who finds his way to these Parnassian islands.
A swan goes by head low with many apologies,
Fantastic light looks through the eyes of bridges –
And look! a barge comes bringing from Athy
And other far-flung towns mythologies.
O commemorate me with no hero-courageous
Tomb – just a canal-bank seat for the passer-by.

This sonnet was written in the mid-1950s, during what Kavanagh called his 'rebirth', a tranquil period of a year or two that followed a serious brush with cancer. The poems from this time were deeper, wiser, gentler than before; they embodied his new detachment, a happy realisation that his 'purpose in life was to have no purpose'.

Kavanagh's wish to be remembered 'where there is water' would be respected. Close to Baggot Street Bridge, not far from where he lived in Pembroke Road, there is now an oak memorial bench on the canal-bank, opposite another in bronze where you can sit beside the poet, or rather beside John Coll's fine lifesize statue of him, wait (probably in vain) for a barge from Athy, and 'let the waters lap idly on the shores of [your] mind'.

from *Mnemosyne Lay in Dust*

Austin Clarke

Past the house where he was got
In darkness, terrace, provision shop,
Wing-hidden convent opposite,
Past public-houses at lighting-up
Time, crowds outside them – Maurice Devane
Watched from the taxi window in vain
National stir and gaiety
Beyond himself: St Patrick's Day,
The spike-ends of the Blue Coat school,
Georgian houses, ribald gloom
Rag-shadowed by gaslight, quiet pavements
      Moon-waiting in Blackhall Place. [. . .]

Cabs ranked at Kingsbridge Station, Guinness
Tugs moored at their wooden quay, glinting
Of Liffey mudbank; hidden vats
Brewing intoxication, potstill,
Laddering of distilleries
Ready to sell their jollities,
Delirium tremens. Dublin swayed,
Drenching, drowning the shamrock: unsaintly
Mirth. The high departments were filed,
Yard, store, unlit. Whiskey-all-round,
Beyond the wealth of that square mile,
      Was healthing every round.

The eighteenth-century hospital
Established by the tears of Madam

Steevens, who gave birth, people said, to
A monster with a pig's snout, pot-head.
The Ford turned right, slowed down. Gates opened,
Closed with a clang; acetelyne glow
Of headlights. How could Maurice Devane
Suspect from weeping-stone, porch, vane,
The classical rustle of the harpies,
Hopping in filth among the trees,
The Mansion of Forgetfulness
Swift gave us for a jest ?

These lines are taken from the beginning of an accomplished
long poem that was published when Austin Clarke (1896–1974)
was seventy. They look back almost fifty years to the day he was
admitted to St Patrick's Mental Hospital after a nervous break-
down. In the third verse above Clarke pointedly alludes to the
fact that the 'Mansion of Forgetfulness' was a legacy to Ireland
from Jonathan Swift – as the Dean mentions in the obituary of
himself that appears in 'Verses on the Death of Doctor Swift', an
extraordinary poem he wrote fourteen years before he died:

He gave what little wealth he had
To build a house for fools and mad;
And show'd by one satiric touch,
No nation wanted it so much:
That kingdom he hath left his debtor,
I wish it soon may have a better.

Austin Clarke's literary career was a varied and somewhat
anguished one, and his talent was initially dominated and
obscured by the long shadow of W. B. Yeats. In the 1930s the
young Samuel Beckett unaccountably took against him, and his

novel *Murphy* (1938) poked hilarious but very cruel fun at him under the transparent disguise of 'Austin Ticklepenny', an alcoholic, homosexual 'pot-poet' from Dublin, who despite a 'pretentious fear of going mad' has taken a job in a mental home. Clarke was narrowly dissuaded from pursuing a libel action, but was to publish no further poetry until he returned with a new anger and satirical edge seventeen years later.

Bloomsday 1976

Seán Críonna Mac Seóinín

Today is Bloomsday! Drink, rejoice and sing,
For Dedalus never flew upon one wing.

Let's go back, if we can, to Dublin past,
To Smyllie, Bang-bang, Myles and Gainor Crist,
And if we drink until the barrel's empty
We could get back as far as 1920!

How nice it is to booze here till we're beggared
And reminisce, remembering how we staggered
From Searson's to McDaid's with Paddy Kavanagh . . .
– But did he ever ask us, 'Whatcha havin'?'

Ah, I resented that, but now I find
It isn't Paddy's poverty I mind
But all those College critics who presume
(They hated him alive) to say they knew him.

We'll have another pint, and try to bring
Back nights when Brendan Behan used to sing
With me and you and Ryan and our cronies
In Davy Byrne's and Neary's and Moroney's.

And were you there when Dublin's greatest joke
Was Cecil Salkeld painted buff with puke?
What wit we had, what poetry! The shame is –
If we'd published any we'd be famous.

But then, the works of literature we offered
Were talked into the air, not sold for profit.
You never wrote too much yourself, did you?
And nor did I. One day I'm planning to.

Today is Bloomsday! Drink, rejoice and fall:
Dedalus never really flew at all.

For those of us who were young in Dublin in the 1970s, there
was a distinct sense of being surrounded by eminent ghosts. You
could meet talkative men in pubs who had drunk (or as some-
one more accurately put it, had been drunk) with Brendan
Behan or Flann O'Brien. Even then we were aware that this
sense of a looming past, full of extraordinary personalities, was
nothing new. As the late John Ryan, a convivial literary Jack-of-
all-Trades (he had once owned the Bailey Tavern in Duke Street)
wrote in his 1975 memoir, *Remembering How We Stood*:

> Dublin was a town of 'characters' then as now, and I suppose
> will ever be. A man I knew was taking a stroll down Grafton
> Street one day when he happened to overhear part of a
> discussion which three citizens were having outside
> Mitchell's café. The gist of their dialogue was that they were
> deploring the absence from the Dublin scene of any *real*
> 'characters'. They appeared to be genuinely aggrieved. They
> were, in fact, Myles na gCopaleen, Sean O'Sullivan and
> Brendan Behan.

It was not only Dublin's poets like Austin Clarke who had
difficulty wriggling out from under the burden that their

illustrious forebears had placed upon them: prose writers suffered too, particularly those who admired James Joyce and despaired of ever finding a voice of their own. It seemed at first that matters were becoming even worse when everyone began to celebrate Bloomsday, the day upon which Joyce had set *Ulysses*. Suddenly, every June 16th, the novel surreally sprang to life in a parody of itself. Tourists flocked to Dublin to gape at multiple versions of Leopold Bloom and Stephen Dedalus, each with his respective bowler hat or aesthete's ashplant, as they sauntered around town, or along Sandymount Strand, generally in the company of bronzed ladies clad in the garb of Edwardian hoydens.

But time went by, and things changed, and Dublin changed, and during the 1980s and 1990s and 2000s new generations of writers came to realise that they already possessed their own voices, fresh, mature, unafraid. These men and women did not feel, as their predecessors so often had, that to be real writers they would have to leave the country. Perhaps the most welcome sign of all was when Seamus Heaney, from the Ulster county of Derry across the border, came to live in Dublin. At last, here was a poet for the whole island, a writer to face Yeats and Joyce, and all that long, contradictory past, head on . . .

The Strand

Seamus Heaney

The dotted line my father's ashplant made
On Sandymount Strand
Is something else the tide won't wash away.

Acknowledgements

We would like to thank the following for granting us permission to use poems still in copyright:

'Enueg I' by Samuel Beckett, from *Collected Poems* (Calder, London, 1984) by permission of Faber & Faber Ltd; verses from 'Mnemosyne Lay in Dust' by Austin Clarke, from *MlinD* (P. Dolmen, Dublin, 1966) by permission of R. Dardis Clarke, 7 Oscar Square, Dublin 8, rdc@eircom.net; 'Liffey Bridge' by Oliver St John Gogarty, from *The Poems & Plays of Oliver St John Gogarty* edited by A. N. Jeffares (Colin Smythe, Gerrards Cross, 2001) by permission of Colin Smythe Limited, on behalf of V. J. O'Mara; 'The Strand' by Seamus Heaney, from *The Spirit Level* (Faber & Faber, London, 1996) by permission of Faber & Faber Ltd; the poems and extracts from poems by Patrick Kavanagh are reprinted from *Collected Poems*, edited by Antoinette Quinn (Allen Lane, 2004), by kind permission of the Trustees of the Estate of the late Katherine B. Kavanagh, through the Jonathan Williams Literary Agency; 'Dublin' by Louis MacNeice, from 'The Closing Album I', in *Collected Poems* (Faber & Faber, London, 1966) by permission of David Higham Associates; 'Nelson Street' by Seumas O'Sullivan, from the *Oxford Book of Irish Verse*, edited by L. Robinson & D. MacDonogh (Oxford University Press, Oxford, 1958) by permission of Frances Sommerville; 'Bag-Snatching in Dublin' by Stevie Smith, from *Selected Poems* (Penguin, London) by permission of the Estate of James MacGibbon; 'Beautiful Lofty Things' by W. B. Yeats, from *Collected Poems*, by permission of A. P. Watt Ltd on behalf of Gráinne Yeats.

Every effort has been made to trace or contact copyright holders. The publishers would be pleased to rectify any omissions brought to their notice at the earliest opportunity.

Index of poem titles

Index of poets

Index of first lines